P9-ELQ-953

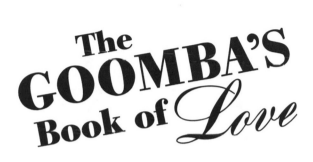

The
GOOMBA'S
Book of *Love*

Also by STEVEN R. SCHIRRIPA
and Charles Fleming

A Goomba's Guide to Life

The GOOMBA'S Book of *Love*

How to LOVE Like a Guy from the Neighborhood

Steven R. Schirripa
and CHARLES FLEMING

CLARKSON POTTER/PUBLISHERS
NEW YORK

Copyright © 2003 by Noelani, Inc. and Charles Fleming

All rights reserved. No part of this book may be reproduced or transmitted in any form or by any means, electronic or mechanical, including photocopying, recording, or by any information storage and retrieval system, without permission in writing from the publisher.

Published by Clarkson Potter/Publishers, New York, New York. Member of the Crown Publishing Group, a division of Random House, Inc. www.randomhouse.com

CLARKSON N. POTTER is a trademark and POTTER and colophon are registered trademarks of Random House, Inc.

Printed in the United States of America

Design by Maggie Hinders

Library of Congress Cataloging-in-Publication Data available upon request.

ISBN 1-4000-5089-8

10 9 8 7 6 5 4 3 2 1

First Edition

To the loves of my life:

Laura, Bria, and Ciara

&

for three lovely Goomba-ettes:

Chris, Lori, and Joanne

ACKNOWLEDGMENTS

STEVE SCHIRRIPA would like to thank, for their invaluable help in making this book possible, Alexandria Addams, Diego Aldana, Bernie Allen, Leigh Ann Ambrosi, Louie Anderson, Frank Anobile Sr., Frank Anobile Jr., Mike Anobile Sr., Mike Anobile Jr., The Anobile Family, Ted Arneault, Valerie Baugh, Toby Becker, Joy Behar, Erin Bix, Pat Bolino, Mitchell Burgess, Vito Cap, John Capotoro, David Chalfy, David Chase, Dominic Chianese, Diane Costello, Michael De Georgio, Nick Di Paolo, Carmine Esposito Sr., Carmine Esposito Jr., Ray Favero, Bob Fiandra, The Fiandra Family, Hugh Fink, Robert Funaro, James Gandolfini, Joseph R. Gannascoli, Laurie Gomez, Robin Green, Roger Haber, Mike Hernandez, Mike Harriot, Richie and Anthony Iocolano, Kevin James, Jodi Kirschner, Pam Krauss, Ilene Landress, Don Learned, George Lons, Bill Mahr, John Manfrellotti, Scott Manners, Joe Marzella, John Mascali, Guido Maurino, Johnnyboy Mazzone, Rich and Cathy McElory, Cheryl McLean, Charlie Melfi, Jerry Miner, Linda Moncrief, Vinnie Montalto, Charles Najjar, Judge Nancy Oesterle, Joe Pantoliano, Lisa Perkins, Cecile Cross-Plummer, The Raya Family, Gerry Rindells, Willie Rizzo, Chris Rock, Rocky from Mulberry Street, Rita Rudner, Chuck Sack, Natalie Sarraf, Richard Scanlon, Lorraine Schirripa, Ralph Schirripa, Jeff Singer, Tony Sirico, Hal Spear, Tim Stone, Jeff Sussman, Angela Tarantino, Teddy D., Bob Vannucci, Steven Van Zandt, John Ventimiglia, David Vigliano, Patricia Weber, Bill Westerman, Terry Winter, Barb Wolf, Premiere Caterers, Il Cortile Restaurant, all his friends at the Riviera Hotel and Casino, the entire cast and crew of "The Sopranos," all his friends back in Bensonhurst, his wife Laura and daughters Ciara and Bria, and everyone who helped (you know who you are).

CHARLES FLEMING would like to thank David Vigliano, Pam Krauss, and his wife Julie Singer and daughters Katherine and Frances.

CONTENTS

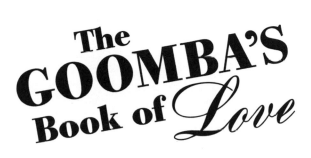

The
GOOMBA'S
Book of *Love*

INTRODUCTION

The goomba is a lovin' man. The one thing he understands, better than anything else in the world except for maybe food, is love. The goomba is practically made of love. His entire life is about love—family love, romantic love, brotherly love, motherly love. He loves his wife—and his *goomar*. He loves his children and his parents. He loves his car and his clothes. He loves to eat and drink and fool around. As a friend, as a father, as a husband, as a lover, the goomba is a big, bubbling, oozing, overflowing . . . well, you get the idea. The goomba is just full of love.

The non-goombas out there may not understand this. They look at the average goomba and what do they see? A big guy, a big appetite, a lot of noise, a certain level of violence, all of it flavored with garlic and tomato sauce on a bed of macaroni. They're missing the point. All that bigness—the big appetite, the big noise and yelling, the big food—that's all about love, too.

If you missed my first book, *A Goomba's Guide to Life,* this might be confusing. You might not even know what a "goomba" is. You're

Goombas don't work alone.

thinking: wiseguy, goodfella, mobbed up, made man, mafia don, whatever. You might think "goomba" is an insult, like "greaseball" or "guinea" or "wop." That ain't it.

Goomba is a term of endearment. It's used to describe an Italian-American man of a certain type. He's probably from the East Coast. He's probably third- or fourth-generation American. He's got a name that ends in a vowel. He works a blue-collar job. He's loyal, stubborn, and patriotic. He idolizes Frank Sinatra. He drives a Cadillac or a Lincoln Town Car. He's a flashy dresser, even when he's wearing nothing but a track suit and a tasteful layer of gold chains. The goomba isn't a college professor, but he's no dummy either.

If you live in New York, New Jersey, or Nevada, you've probably seen lots of goombas out and about. You've probably seen the goomba in action. Because they got a lot of goombas there, and there's a lot of action. The average goomba is always looking for love, one way or another. He might be looking for the love of his life, for the girl he's going to make his wife. He might already be married, in which case he's looking for a *goomar* for the time when he's not with his wife. He might just be looking for sex. But he's always looking.

He's probably not traveling alone. The goomba don't work alone. He's in a group of three or four guys, or more. They're out having a drink, having a meal, watching the game, laying down a few bets or whatever. But out of the corner of their eyes, they're also checking out the broads. This is one of the defining characteristics of the goomba. They are always, no matter what else they're doing, checking out the broads. A goomba could be on his deathbed, but I guarantee you he's looking at the nurse and thinking, "I could nail her." He could be in court staring at life-without-possibility, but you just know he's thinking, "She's not bad looking—for a judge. I wonder if she wears panties under that robe." When the goomba gets to heaven, the first thing he says to St. Peter is, "So, how's the action around here?"

If you're not from one of those goomba capitals, or you're not sure whether the guys you're looking at are true goombas, pay attention to the way they talk. Goombas say, and don't say, certain things.

Things you'll always hear a goomba say:
"Yo, Vinnie!"
"I made him an offer he couldn't refuse."
"Let's eat."

On the other hand, there's things that a goomba just couldn't say.

Things you'll never hear a goomba say:
"Checkmate."
"Two Pink Ladys for me and my friend, bartender."
"Where the fuck did I put my cowboy hat?"

If you're still confused about what is and what is not a goomba, here's a little refresher course.

You might be a goomba if:

You've ever eaten a sandwich on the toilet.

The photo in your high school yearbook was your mug shot.

You own a VCR, a CD player, and a DVD player, but you've never been in a store that sells these items.

Your mother's apartment has a framed picture of Frank Sinatra on the wall, next to one of Jesus Christ.

You can't be a goomba if:

You pay taxes.

You vote.

You listen to country music.

You shop at Old Navy.

You ever sat in the cheap seats.

Still confused? Here are some more guidelines.

You're probably not a goomba if:

You've ever said, "Pass the Velveeta."

You've ever said, "Is Oprah on yet?"

You knit.

You know anyone who knits.

You ever said to your wife, "Sit down and let *me* do the dishes."

On the other hand, you're *definitely* a goomba if:

You'd rather starve than eat a Domino's pizza.

You'd rather starve than eat anything made by Ragu.

You'd rather starve than eat at The Olive Garden.
You have a middle name that starts with "The."
You know a guy who knows a guy.

Above all, the goomba is passionate. Everything he does—whether it's cooking dinner, chasing women, or placing a bet with his bookie—he does with feeling. He's quick to fight, quick to forgive, and just as quick to fall in love.

How do I know? I'm a goomba! I grew up surrounded by goombas. All my best friends are goombas. All my heroes are goombas.

So believe me when I tell you this: Boil it all down, and the bottom line on the goomba is . . . love.

Consider *The Godfather.* Look at the love in that family. Everything that happens in that story is about love—Don Corleone's love for his sons, Michael's love for his father, and everybody's love for power and money.

Look at *The Sopranos.* What is that show really about? Love! The love of family and family honor. Carmela's love for Tony. Tony's love for Carmela. And everybody's love for baked ziti and gabagool.

Look at the lyrics to the famous song: "When the moon hits your eye, like a big pizza pie . . . that's *amore.*" It's practically the goomba national anthem, as sung by that great goomba Dean Martin (real name, Dino Crocetti), and what's it called? *"Amore"!* Again with the love!

Here's the average goomba: He's got a big family, brothers and sisters, cousins and aunts and uncles, a bunch of kids, a wife, and two or maybe three girlfriends on the side. He needs a lot of love! Because he's got a lot of love to give.

He expresses it in all kinds of ways. The loving goomba father says things to his kids, like

"Finish your dinner, or there'll be no gun for Christmas."

"Never mind whose bike it is. Just enjoy it."

"If your buddy Tony shot someone and threw him off a bridge, I suppose you'd do that, too?"

The loving goomba boyfriend does crazy things when he's in love, like stealing flowers from the cemetery, or actually obeying the restraining order. The loving goomba husband never lets his wife catch him cheating on her with his girlfriend—because that would hurt her feelings. The really loving goomba husband buys a diamond ring for his wife that's even bigger than the one he bought for himself.

In my first book, *A Goomba's Guide to Life*, I explained how to live like a guy from the neighborhood—how to walk, talk, and dress like a goomba, how to tip a maitre d', how to behave at a funeral, how to cook a plate of macaroni. But I think maybe the best lesson you can take away from any goomba is how to *love* like a guy from the neighborhood—how to be the best goomba boyfriend, husband, parent, son, or friend you can be.

Is goomba love really so different from, say, Puerto Rican love, or suburban love, or cowboy love? You bet.

To the non-goomba, *everything* about goomba love is probably going to be confusing. Because, vice versa, everything about non-goomba love is confusing to the goomba.

For example, the personal ads. No goomba would ever try and meet a girl through the personal ads. If you're a goomba, you meet a girl through people you know. You have to be able to check her out. You have to know about her family. For most goombas, this is easy. Most goombas wind up marrying girls they've known for years—neighborhood girls, where you know their brothers and their parents and all their friends before you even go out.

With the personals, what is that? It's like buying a used car.

From a crooked dealer. Because you know no one is telling the truth in those ads. I see some of the ones they have today and I have to laugh. They have these categories: "Celebrity I Resemble Most." Apparently all men resemble Harrison Ford, Ben Affleck, or Brad Pitt, and all women resemble Cameron Diaz, Jennifer Lopez, or Julia Roberts. Then you look at the pictures next to the ads, and you think, "He looks like Quasimodo. She looks like Moby Dick."

If the goomba ran an ad, the answers would be a little different:

OCCUPATION: I'm in the construction and sanitation business.

CELEBRITY I RESEMBLE MOST: Half Robert De Niro, half Al Pacino. Some Ben Affleck.

LAST GREAT BOOK I READ: *Bookmaking for Dummies.*

IN MY BEDROOM YOU'LL FIND: One Glock, one baseball bat, a half-empty jar of Vaseline, cannoli crumbs, and me with a hard-on, baby!

FIVE ITEMS I CAN'T LIVE WITHOUT: Garlic, my Cadillac, my bookie's cell phone number, my gold chains, and crushed red pepper.

Who would answer an ad like that? Actually, a lot of goomba-ettes. They know a goomba when they see one, and they like what they see.

And they're not wrong. Because a goomba in love is a powerful force. The way he loves his mother, his kids, his women—the wife and anyone else he may be doing on the side—the way he loves his capacola sandwich—it's something no one should get in the way of. It's a beautiful thing.

The following chapters will show you how to make *amore* the goomba way. When you're done, you'll be like Barry White—deep, wide, and full of love—but probably still white.

CHAPTER
1

First Love:
A Goomba and
His Mother

Nothing is more powerful than a mother's love. That is why mothers are so difficult to live with.

$\mathcal{T}$he mother is the most important force in every boy's life, but this is especially true in the Italian community and in the goomba household. The mother is king, queen, president, and dictator. The goomba loves his mother more than he will ever love another human being until he has children.

Nothing is more powerful than a mother's love. That is why mothers are so difficult to live with. In my house, when I was a kid, my mother ran everything. That's partly because my dad was a screw-up. He was a bookie, and a gambler, and a ladies' man, and he wasn't around all that much. But it was also partly because my mother was one tough broad, and she knew how to run a household.

She ruled with an iron fist. No, that's not true. She ruled with a wooden spoon. This was her weapon of choice. Some families it's a dad with a belt. In my house, if you got out of line, you got the wooden spoon.

One time, I was about 17 or 18, and I stayed out all night. I'd been out with some people, and it was morning before I got home. I came in wearing the same clothes I was wearing the night before. My mother came after me with the wooden spoon, screaming. "Where have you been? Who were you with? You're a *whoo-ah!* Nothing but a *whoo-ah!*"

All the time, she's battin' me over the head with this big wooden spoon. I had Sunday sauce all over me by the time she was done.

This is tough love. It comes from having a tough life—and my mother had a tough life. My father wasn't around. She was raising five kids. On her own. On welfare, and working a job on the side. She got sixty bucks a month for cleaning up at the local Democratic Club. They'd rent the hall out for parties, and then my mother would come in and mop the floors and scrub the toilets. And we still didn't have enough money, partly because my mother refused to move out of the neighborhood. We couldn't afford a good apartment in Brooklyn, but she refused to move to the projects or to some crummy neighborhood with no Italians. So, we stayed in a good neighborhood, in Bensonhurst, all six of us crammed into this two-bedroom apartment on Bay 11th Street. My mother clawed and struggled, and why? For the love of her kids.

I come from two generations of tough mothers, now that I think about it. My grandmother was tough, too—especially on my grandfather. I think they hated each other. They had an arranged marriage. They were both Calabrese, from the same little town. He was older, and he'd been married before and his first wife had died. Now he's married to my grandmother, and they come to America. She's got two brothers. She loves these guys! They live with her and her husband. She cooks for them, and treats them

My grandmother and grandfather.

nice, and everything. For my grandfather, nothing. She won't even cook for him. He has to take his meals in a restaurant, while she's at home cooking for her brothers.

He was like this old Italian guy I heard a story about. This guy was dying. He was on his deathbed. He knew his number was up. But as he lay there preparing to meet his maker, he starts to smell this unbelievable smell. Something incredible is coming from the kitchen. He thinks he's died and gone to heaven already, it smells so good. So he gathers all his strength and

A goomba mom.

gets up from his deathbed. He goes toward the smell. All he can think is, "My wonderful wife has made a delicious meal to serve me before I die! What a lovely woman!"

He finally makes it into the dining room. What does he see? His wife's meatballs! In Sunday sauce! His favorite meal in all the world! He reaches for a taste of this heavenly food, and picks up a meatball and puts it to his lips—when suddenly his wife comes out of nowhere and smacks him on the hand with a big wooden spoon.

"Drop it!" she yells. "Those are for the funeral!"

My grandfather was a sweet old guy. Every time he saw me in the street he'd give me a quarter—which in those days was pretty good money. Sometimes, me and my friends would go looking for him. "Let's go find my grandfather and get a quarter!" We'd usually find him at the bocci court. He'd give us money and we'd go buy potato chips. I was his favorite grandchild.

That's tough love. It starts early. There's a lot of screaming and yelling and smacking going on between the goomba mother and her children. More than in other cultures. When my wife and I first got married, we came to New York. She went to the market. All she saw was these goomba mothers with their children, shopping in groups of threes and fours. And all of them were screaming the whole time and smacking their children. "Anthony, stop it!" Smack. "Angelo, get over here!" Smack.

She came back to the apartment and said, "You won't believe what I saw at the market."

I said, "Welcome to my life."

Whenever my family would get together on Sunday, she'd say, "Don't you people ever stop yelling?"

I'd say, "Only when we eat."

The goomba mother's love is complete, and unconditional. Goomba parents love their children more than anything in the world. But it's a firm love. There are limits to what the goomba mother is going to take. You can hear this in what they say, and what they don't say. Here are some things you will never hear.

Things a goomba mother will never say to her daughter:
"That boyfriend of yours is some rapper!"
"You're right. You don't need a bra with that dress."
"Benjamin Goldberg, welcome to the family!"

Things a goomba mother will never say to her son:
"Shawanna seems like a nice girl."
"Why Yale? I think Harvard's English department is stronger."
"You and Todd make a lovely couple."

The emotions run high in the goomba household. No one talks anything out. If there's a problem, there's going to be some action, now. Yelling, screaming, slapping, *something*. Now.

But tough as she is, the goomba mother loves her son in a special way. To the goomba mother, a son can do no wrong. Whatever happened, it wasn't his fault. If he's in trouble, he didn't do it. She'll swear on a stack of Bibles that he's innocent. He was home the whole time!

If he gets in trouble with a girl, it was the girl's fault—always. Go into a goomba neighborhood. Sooner or later you'll hear two mothers screaming at each other:

"Your son got my daughter pregnant!"

"It's because she has her legs open all the time, the *whoo-ah*."

"But they have three children together!"

"That's what I mean—with her legs open all the time!"

I didn't get in all that much trouble when I was a kid, but my mother was always there trying to bail me out. For example, I used to get parking tickets. My mother would take them away from me, and write a check. This woman was still mopping floors for sixty bucks a month! But she'd write the check. And then she'd say, "Don't tell your father."

The goomba mother will never take anyone's side against her child—not even her husband's. In most goomba households, the mother will take her child's side every time. Many a goomba has heard his mother scream at his father, "Don't you touch my child!"

Sometimes that kind of protective instinct gets carried away. I remember once in my street these two kids got into a tussle. They were about six. One of the kid's mothers came outside and started yelling. She called the other kid a "monster." He ran home and told his mother. She went directly to the other mother's apartment and started banging on the door. The other mother wouldn't unlock the door. So this kid's mom smashed her hand through the glass and opened the door herself. She's screaming, "You come out here and apologize to my son!" with so much blood pouring out of her that she looks like she's dying. She got the apology and then went to the emergency room to get stitched up.

Even if he is caught red-handed, the goomba mother defends her son. There was a story in the papers not long ago. This Italian guy threatened to blow up an airplane in France. He said he was a terrorist and that he had a bomb. The plane made an emergency landing and the cops grabbed the guy. It turns out he didn't have a bomb, and he wasn't a terrorist. But he *was* crazy, and dangerous. He had already tried to hijack another French plane in 1999, and had hijacked an Italian train in 1998. He'd been in and out of the nut house.

The police contacted his family. They told his mother exactly what had happened. What was his mother's response?

She said, "Oh, no! He's done it again! I've been anxious for hours because he didn't come home for lunch."

This is a classic goomba mother! Her son is a psychotic, serial hijacker of passenger jets and trains, but he's still living at home, and his mother gets worried when he's late for lunch. She's not even worried about the hijacking stuff. She just wants to know should she keep his lunch hot, or start making dinner.

A goomba mother will do anything for her children. No sacrifice is too big. She'll scrimp and save, work two jobs, lie and steal, anything! She's going to take care of the family, or die. Nothing is too much.

For example, we were very poor when I was growing up. No money. No father to support us. My mother would send us to the market with little notes for the grocer, promising to pay him back if he could just let us have some things on account. Or, worse, we would go and pick up welfare food. We were on the food stamp program, and once a month we were also given free food. It was all inedible. They'd give us these huge blocks of government cheese—big yellow bricks of this tasteless, odorless junk. We were the only family on the block on welfare. We were the only family I knew that had eggs for dinner—because it was the only thing in the house you could cook for dinner. We had welfare eggs.

My mother would send me to the market with the food stamps, to buy food. By the time I was a teenager, I couldn't do it anymore. It was too embarrassing. I was 13, and I said, "Everybody in the neighborhood knows me. I can't go into the market with food stamps!" I refused. To this day, I can't go into the supermarket with a coupon.

It was embarrassing for us not to have money. But somehow we always had what we needed. We always had Christmas presents. We always had birthday presents. We always had clean clothes—even if they were usually hand-me-downs. I do remember having to wear tennis shoes with holes in the soles. I had to put pieces of cardboard in there to keep from wearing holes in my socks, too. And I remember having the electricity turned off sometimes. Looking back now, that seems pretty bad. How much could it cost to keep the electricity going? A few bucks? But we didn't have it.

But it didn't stop us from doing the things we wanted to do. I wanted to be in Little League, but we couldn't afford the uniform. Or the equipment. But somehow my mother made it happen. She hustled it. She called the church and said, "My son wants to play ball, but we can't afford the uniform." So we got a uniform for free. She told someone else the same story, and I got a glove. This must have been hard on her dignity, to go begging to the church. But she did it.

She got us into all kinds of programs that way. Every summer, we'd go away to camp, to this place called IBG—the Italian Board of Guardians. It was for underprivileged Italian kids. It was in upstate New York. She managed to get all us kids in there, year after year.

One year, I was playing ball. I was about nine. At the end of the season, I was picked for the all-star team. What an honor! This was the greatest thing that had ever happened to me. But there was a problem. The all-star game was going to be played on a Tuesday, at the beginning of the summer. And summer camp at IBG started on

Monday. My mother had pulled some strings to get me into the camp. There was no way I wasn't going. But she also knew how important this all-star game was.

So she called the camp and said I was sick. On Tuesday night, I was in the all-star game. On Wednesday morning, she left all my brothers and sisters home, alone, and took me to camp. We took the train from Brooklyn into Manhattan, to the Port Authority. We got a Greyhound bus from there to upstate New York. We rode about three hours, to the town where the camp was. She dropped me off at the camp, kissed me goodbye, and then went back to the Greyhound station. It was three or four hours back, then the train back into Brooklyn.

This was eight or ten hours of traveling for her—just so her son could play in the Little League all-star game. And this was a woman that had hardly ever left the city before. This wasn't some world traveler who just hops on a bus every day. I don't think she had ever been upstate, even. She had never been out of New York, except to New Jersey. She had never been in an airplane until I flew her out to Las Vegas, almost twenty years later. The only time she had ever stayed in a hotel room until then was on her honeymoon.

It wasn't like we all took family vacations. For us, going to Manhattan would have been a vacation. I remember my mother took us to the World's Fair in 1964. I was about seven. She had five kids already. She put us on the bus and schlepped us into Queens because she thought we should all see the World's Fair. It was a great day.

For a holiday, we went to Coney Island. We'd get up early, pack everything up, take the bus to Coney Island and get there around noon. We'd spend the whole day on the beach. My mother would pack our lunch and our dinner. We'd eat sandwiches for both meals. We'd stay until it got dark, then lie in the sand and watch the fireworks. We wouldn't get home until midnight. That was a vacation, for my family. And it was all thanks to my mother's efforts.

It wasn't just when I was a kid, either. My mother put her dignity on the line and kept making things happen until me and my sisters were grown up. She called people. She got things done. Whatever it was, she always said, "We can do this." She didn't have much education herself—she went to high school, and she went to nursing school—but she knew education was important. She didn't think her kids should be deprived of an education just because we didn't have money.

So, she got my sister into this exclusive school in Connecticut. I don't know how, but she got on the phone and started making calls. She got my sister admitted to this school, with all kinds of grants and financial aid.

She even busted her ass to try and get me into Poly Prep. This is a great school, right in Brooklyn. Beautiful campus, been there a hundred years, a real diamond in the rough, so to speak. I wanted to go to school there, but of course we couldn't afford it. So my mother started making calls. Next thing you know, she's got me a half-scholarship and a financial aid package. Unbelievable. Unfortunately, I didn't do well enough on the admissions test to get in. But she did her part.

My mother would do anything for her kids. But to this day, she still thinks everyone is better than her because they have money. When I was a kid, I'd see something going on in the neighborhood, like someone riding a new bike, or someone's dad driving a new car, and she'd say, "What do you expect? They have money." I'd say, "He's a mailman." She'd say, "Believe me, they have money." Like they inherited millions. Like someone, somewhere had cheated her out of hers.

It turns out, she had a reason to feel this way. I didn't know until I was older, but she was adopted. And her natural father was a Jewish wiseguy.

Four Sopranos and my mom

He was a member of Murder Inc., the Jewish mafia. He was a very dangerous guy, and a very dapper guy, and a very wealthy guy. No one knows who his girlfriend was, but he was fooling around with someone and he got her pregnant. He didn't want to marry her. The baby was born out of wedlock. The name listed for the mother on the birth certificate is Helen Smith. Like Jane Doe. My mother was born without a mother.

The wiseguy raised my mother on his own for a little while. Then he met and married a girl named Sally Moskowitz. Not too long after that he died, and things went south. Here comes the Depression. There goes the money. Pretty soon Sally is struggling. She goes from being a gangster's moll to being a factory worker. My mother gets sent out to a series of foster homes. For a while, she doesn't know where she's living from one month to the next.

Then Sally meets and marries a guy named Joe. My mother gets to come home. They set up house in Bensonhurst. My mother is being raised by two people who aren't really her parents, now, but things are stable. She thinks of Sally as her mother and Joe as her stepfather. And she believes, in the back of her mind, that her rich gangster *real* father has left her a pile of money somewhere, and that someday she's going to get it and never have to worry about being poor again.

That didn't happen. Instead, she met my father. When I say her life was never easy, I mean it was *never* easy. For a couple of years, maybe, it's not miserable. She and my father have a couple of laughs. They go dancing a lot. He's a good-looking guy and a nice dresser and they're both good dancers. They get married over the objections of his family when she's 21 and he's only 18.

Things are okay, for maybe two or three years. My father had a legit job, doing something for the company that made Beechnut gum. Then the wiseguy stuff started. First it's little petty stuff on the side. Then it's bookmaking on the side. Then it's all he's doing. For the next twenty years, he never has a real job. He's doing petty criminal stuff, and getting arrested, and getting put in jail. He's having to run upstate and disappear for months at a time. He's gambling away whatever money he does make. There's never any security of any kind. No one knows where the next nickel is coming from.

And the kids are arriving like trains at Penn Station. My sister Donna is born in 1951. My sister Diane is born in 1954. I'm born in 1957. My brother Richard is born in 1961. My sister Doreen comes last in 1962.

My mother used to say, "Your father's pants could be hanging over the back of the chair and I'd get pregnant."

My mother was born in 1928. My sister Doreen was born in 1962. That means my mother was 34 years old, with five children, with no husband, and no money, living in a two-bedroom apartment in Bensonhurst, trying to hold this all together on her own. How's a goomba not gonna love a woman like that? And that's what he'll expect from *his* wife, too.

The average goomba kid, unfortunately, doesn't do much to help out. He's doing the best he can. But it ain't that good. For example:

- ♥ A goomba kid's idea of helping with the housework is lifting his feet so his mother can vacuum underneath.
- ♥ A goomba kid's idea of dressing up for company is combing his hair.
- ♥ A goomba kid's idea of being polite means not scratching his ass while guests are talking to him.
- ♥ A goomba kid's idea of helping clean up after dinner is leaving the room.

But even if the goomba kid isn't out mowing lawns to help with the family budget, to his mother, he's a hero. And they share a closeness you won't find in a lot of families.

My mom.

When I was growing up, my mother knew everything about me. I told her everything. She knew who I was friends with, what we did, who I was dating, even who I was fooling around with. You might think a goomba would never discuss sex with his mother— wrong. She not only talks about it, she practically participates vicariously.

My mother, she'd look at a picture, or point at a girl in the street, and say, "Her?" And I'd say, "Yeah, Ma. I'm giving her a little."

Goomba guys do this. My friend Mike remembers that as a kid his family used to spend a week every summer at the Pleasant View Lodge in the Catskills. That's where he fell in love for the first time. Her name was Camille. Mike was 12 or 13 years old. He fell hard. One night, he saw Camille flirting with this other guy. He was crushed. Devastated. Ruined. He went to his mother and told her what had happened. His mother said, "She flirted with another boy? She's a *puttana.* She's no good for you anyway. You can do better than a *whoo-ah* like that."

My friend Frank told me he used to bring girls home to introduce to his mother, when they were back home in Canarsie. He'd bring the girl to the house, and she'd sit with his mother for a few

My friend Frankie when he was just gettin' started.

minutes. After, his mother would say something like, "I don't know, Frankie. That one seems a little sneaky to me." That was it. Frankie would never see her again.

Then he moved to Las Vegas and turned into a player, hitting on every girl he met. He started dating strippers and hookers. Later, he moved his mother and father out to Las Vegas and got them a townhouse right next to his. He kept on bringing girls home to meet his mother, but just as a goof. He'd introduce these strippers, just to shock his mother.

One day he was having coffee with his mom when his cell phone rings. It's this girl he's been seeing. She says she's in the neighborhood. He tells her he's having coffee with his mother, and tells the girl to come over.

Fifteen minutes later, she comes in with a box of pastries. She's wearing a $2000 Donna Karan dress. She's got a $50,000 diamond around her neck. She's beautiful. She has a cup of coffee and then Frank takes her back to his place.

Frank's mother was so impressed. She said, "That was a nice girl, Frankie. I know she's not a stripper. She has too much class. The suit. The jewelry. The pastries. What does she do—real estate?"

Frankie said, "Sort of, Ma. She's a hooker."

Because they are so close, the relationship between the goomba and his mother has its own special rules. For example:

Things a goomba will never say to his mother:
"Guess what? I got married!"
"Actually, I like Mrs. Antonucci's lasagne better than yours."
"Grandchildren? *Fuhgeddaboudit.* I don't want kids."
"I'm tired of these Sunday dinners. Can't we just go to
    McDonalds?"
"You and Dad are divorcing? It's about time!"

This stuff works the other way, too. Goomba mothers are very particular about how they raise their children. Certain things are acceptable. Certain things are not.

Things a goomba mother will never say to her child:
"Your parole officer called. I told him you were out robbing a
    liquor store."
"So you forgot Mother's Day? Big deal!"
"Why should I care whether you marry an Italian girl or not?"
"Do what makes you happy—why should I care what career
    you choose?"

My mother never told me about sex. She never sat me down and explained anything to me. And I was never explicit with her about what I was doing. But she'd joke with me. She'd say, "Don't you get a girl pregnant! Don't you ever get any girl pregnant!" She was joking, but she wasn't joking. That was as much as she could say about it.

For some goombas, this relationship never changes. A lot of

goombas live at home until they get married. And some of them don't get married. Or they don't get married until they're in their forties or fifties. I know some guys who have always lived at home. Their fathers have passed away. Now their mothers wait on *them* hand and foot, like they used to wait on their fathers.

My friend Frank is a very successful guy. He makes over $200,000 a year. He's 43 years old. But his mother still picks up his laundry from her townhouse next door and washes and dries and irons it for him. And he still yells at her if it isn't done properly. Frank's still single, and he's a very active bachelor, and believe me his mother knows everything that goes on in his house! She's washing his shorts! You can't keep any secrets from the woman that washes your underwear.

I have another friend who lives in Queens. He lived with his parents until he was 38 years old. His mother did his laundry and his cooking, and he ate all his meals with his mother and father. Then he met a girl and they got married, and it was time for the goomba to leave the nest. So he bought his own house—on the same street, on the same block, five houses down.

And his brother has a house on the same street, five more houses down the block!

This is not uncommon in the goomba family. They're very close. Sometimes it's even all in one building. I know guys who live in three-story buildings in the neighborhood. It's supposed to be three different houses, but they've fixed it so it's really one house. The main floor is where there's the kitchen and the dining room and that other room—the living room—with all the plastic slipcovers on the furniture where no one ever goes. Upstairs from that are all the bedrooms. Downstairs is the basement apartment. The parents live in the basement apartment. The goomba lives on the main floor, which he shares, of course, with his parents. And upstairs, he

Me and my best man Puddy pondering our future.

shares that with his brother and his brother's wife and family. Everybody eats together, and shares the same telephone, and shares the same bathroom.

This is the big thing with the goomba. Stay close! Everyone is yelling. Everyone is on top of everyone else. There's no such thing as privacy. But you gotta stay close. And it all starts with the mother.

The same kind of thing is true in some Jewish households, and maybe in some Hispanic households. I know some Jewish guys who are in their sixties, but when they're around their mothers they turn into five-year-olds. Mexican guys I know, too, they honor their mother above all other women.

That's a real sign you're a goomba: You weigh 250 pounds and you bench-press 350 pounds and you're so tough you gotta shave twice a day, but you still start crying when your mother yells at you.

Non-goombas, especially guys from the WASP community, won't understand this. I heard a WASP joke once, in fact. This WASP guy calls his mother on the phone. He says, "Mother, I'm sorry, but something has come up. I can't come over for dinner tonight."

And his mother says, "That's okay, dear. *We'll do it another time.*"

Now, in the goomba household, this can never happen. A goomba who calls his mother and says he's not coming for dinner is going to get a terrible beating—over the phone, or in person. His mother may take out a contract on him. She's gonna yell and scream and lay on the guilt so heavy that most goombas wouldn't be able to make the call in the first place. Whatever it is that comes up—*fuhgeddaboudit.* You're going to dinner at your mother's house. Nothing cancels that.

In my first book, I told a story about a guy who was so hard up for money that he hired a couple of goombas to pretend to kidnap him so his mother would pay the ransom. Another guy might have just asked his mother for a loan. Not this guy. He was so scared of his mother—and he was such a slimeball, by the way—that he had these tough guys frighten the money out of her.

That would never happen in a true goomba family. In most goomba families I know, in fact, the money is traveling the other direction. When I see my mother, I always bring a couple *hundge.* I stick a C-note in her hand, just as a way of saying "thanks" and as a way of making sure she's taking care of herself. When I didn't have a hundred, I gave her fifty. If I didn't have fifty to spare, I'd spring a twenty. Some guys I know, they give their mothers five bucks a week. It's the gesture. It shows respect—and love. This is how a proper goomba man, a real man, treats his mother.

Most goombas love their mothers, deep down inside, no matter how crazy their mothers make them. They're always trying to do the right thing. This starts very early in life. The goomba son is always trying to please his goomba mother. I remember my friend Joe telling me about being a kid in Brooklyn. He'd go to church every Sunday, like a good Italian goomba boy. On Mother's Day, the church would have little flowers for sale, in little pots, so that each goomba could take home a present for his mother.

Joe was very poor—probably because he had lost all his money gambling. He didn't have a buck to buy a flower for his mother on Mother's Day.

So he did the natural goomba thing. He stole *two flowers,* in pots, and brought them home to present to his mother.

There are some things, though, that a real goomba can never say to his mother, or do to his mother. You want some evidence, go back and watch the first season of *The Sopranos.* Tony Soprano's mother was the most evil, backstabbing, vicious mother in history— may God rest her soul. At the time of her death, she was getting ready to put a hit on her own son. Her own son! Her first-born baby! And Tony, what could he do? He knew this was going on, but what could he do? Could a goomba man take out a contract on his own mother, even in self-defense? Never!

Any goomba's relationship with his mother can be difficult. Goomba moms are tough. The mom is the boss, when her husband isn't home. She's the disciplinarian. The goomba mom doesn't say, "Wait until your father gets home," unless she's got something to add to that—like, "Wait until your father gets home from jail," or "Wait until your father gets home from the track."

Probably all this stuff is changing now. My generation is the last one that will have this experience. The younger goomba-ettes, they ain't going for all that old-fashioned stuff. A lot of them have an education. A lot of them work. In my mother's time, that was not the case. The father was the breadwinner. He went to work. He brought home the bacon. The mother stayed home and cooked the bacon. When you got home from school in the afternoon, your mother was there. She helped you with the homework while she cooked your dinner. It was very unusual for her to do work outside the home. None of my friends had mothers who worked.

Today, a lot of goomba-ettes have jobs that they keep even after they get married. Some of them cut hair, or sell real estate, or they do

Your mother is probably pretty tough, too. But what are you gonna do? She's your mother! So, you learn to talk to her like a good son even if you don't feel like a good son. Follow these examples, and when you want to strangle her you'll sound like you're sending her flowers.

If she says, "I can't believe you're marrying a stripper."
You say, "Ma, you know you're the only girl I really love."

If she says, "This girl you want to marry. Can she cook?"
You say, "Ma, nobody cooks as good as you."

If she says, "Why don't you get a decent job like your cousin Angie?"
You say, "What? And spend less time with you?"

the books for other businesses. They have real lives, outside the home. My mother had no life outside the home. In fact, she could hardly get outside the home even if she had a life. She never drove a car. She didn't know how. She didn't have a license. My grandmother, too. And, now that I think of it, my sisters, too. I have two sisters that don't drive—don't know how, don't have a license, don't care to learn.

In the old days, they wouldn't need one. Where are you gonna go? Everyone you know, everything you need, every place you have to be—it's all right in the neighborhood. Stay close! That's the goomba way.

And maybe that's why my mother wanted her children to keep living at home, even when we were grown up. She would always tell us she wanted us to continue living at home as long as possible—which was ridiculous. You got two adults, one dog, and five kids, three of them in their twenties, all living in this same apartment. She should have been dying for us to move out. But no. She wanted us all to stay. She even warned us: Once we left—we could never come back. If you moved out to live with a girl, forget it. You never came back to live at home. She must have meant it because no one ever came back after they moved out.

Where I got lucky is I married a goomba mother without even knowing it. My wife isn't even Italian. She's Mexican. But where it counts, she's just like the goomba mother every goomba wishes he had. She's the glue that holds the family together. She's the strength in the relationship. She's the one everybody in the family comes crying to. She's the one who will never take anyone's side against you. No matter what happens, no matter who's done what to who, she's on your side.

Laura and Steve

I know that, when they're grown up, my daughters are going to love their mother the very same way I love mine, no matter how crazy she can make me sometimes. And my daughters are going to grow up to be good mothers too, when their time comes.

Brotherly Love: A
Goomba and His
Buddies

. . . if you're really friends with a guy, you share everything—your money, your food, your car, your girlfriend, whatever.

*N*ow maybe you thought for the goomba that love is all about the opposite sex. You couldn't be more wrong. There's almost nothing more important to a goomba than friendship. A goomba friend is a friend for life. You grow up with a guy, you get to know a guy, you spend some time with a guy... *that's* permanent. Unless a guy turns out to be a rat, or a back-stabber, once he's a friend he's a friend forever. Your best friend from eighth grade is going to be the best man at your wedding, the godfather to your children, and the pallbearer at your funeral.

I'm still close to guys I met in elementary school. We don't live in the same city, or have the same interests, or do the same work, or even know the same people anymore, but when we get together, it's exactly like 1971 in Mrs. Giamela's class all over again. Some of these guys are wiseguys. Some of them, I don't even wanna *know* what they do for a living. But it doesn't matter. We get together, we have a few drinks, we have a few laughs, and it's great. What they do is no business of mine—and vice versa. Sometimes they mention seeing me in a movie, or on a TV show. Usually, they don't. Instead, they give me a good ribbing about the night I lost my virginity, or the time I threw an eraser at the back of Mrs. Giamela's head during the math test.

When I was a teenager, I hung out on the street corner, just like any goomba in every other goomba neighborhood all over the East Coast, with a group of guys. We'd meet, every evening, in front of a drugstore on the corner of 16th and Bath in Bensonhurst. There was

Someday I'll be this size again. I swear.

a bookie on the block where we could place our bets. There was a restaurant across the street that made great sandwiches. There was a grocery store on the other corner where we could buy beer. So we had it all, right on that one corner. You'd get a sandwich, and a quart bottle of Miller or Bud, and you'd place a couple of bets, and you'd hang out with all your friends. (We didn't actually patronize the drugstore itself. Although sometimes, if you had something you needed from the drugstore, you would go inside and "patronize" something into your pocket and then walk out again.)

Every night we'd get together, shoot the breeze, and then go out and do something. Some nights it was dancing. Some nights it was drinking. Some nights we'd go to the track. But every night it was the same ten or twelve guys, goomba pals.

We did everything together. On Saturday afternoons, for example, in preparation for the big Saturday night, a bunch of us would get together and get a shave. We'd meet up and go over to this barber shop run by an old Italian named Jerry. We'd sit in the chairs with the hot towels on our faces while these old Italian barbers sharpened their straight razors on the leather strops. We'd get all lathered up and get a really nice close shave.

We didn't trust our hair to those guys. This was the 1970s, remember. We had special hair. You couldn't get an old-fashioned haircut with the styles we wore. For that you had to go to a salon, where they'd wash your hair and cut it and blow-dry it and turn it into disco hair. But we'd all go together and get that done, too.

I still have the overalls. Too bad they don't fit.

In the later years, we actually got together a little social club. We had our own storefront. We collected dues and paid rent on this place right around the corner from the original hangout. I lived on Bay 11th and Benson. The clubhouse was on Bay 11th and Bath. It had been a store of some kind, maybe a candy store. We turned it into our own space. We brought in a color TV and a pool table and some couches. Guys would come in and drink and hang out. Sometimes guys would bring girls.

Some nights we'd go out drinking. We had a joint we liked a lot called the Sportsman Pub. We'd always have a few drinks there, first, before we'd go out to a club for dancing. Most of the guys would drink a beer or two, or maybe a glass of wine. Sometimes we'd drink shots of tequila. We'd have little contests, to see who could do the most shots without getting stupid. I know some of the guys would try to win by cheating. My friend Richie would often toss his shots over his shoulder, trying to keep up. We all used to kid each other about the drinking. We'd call each other "juicebags."

One night that caused a problem. We were at the Sportsman, as usual. There was this really big guy sitting at the bar—big, like six-foot-seven or so. He bought us some drinks. We bought him some drinks. We all got friendly. My friend Richie toasted him, and said, "You're a real juicebag, just like us!"

The guy was drunk. He didn't hear it right. He jumps up and says, "You called me a douchebag!" And he charges at Richie.

We couldn't allow that to happen. So we nailed him. Somebody broke a glass on his head. Someone else broke a bottle on his head. Someone else broke a chair on his head. Then he went down.

Most of the time, though, we didn't get violent. Sometimes we got stupid. One night, for some reason, we all got angry at the Sportsman. We drove over there in one guy's car and threw a couple of bricks through the bar window.

Unfortunately, there were two off-duty cops drinking there at the time. They came out, saw us taking off, and chased us in their cars. The guy driving our car got confused and went the wrong way down a one-way street. The four of us got handcuffed and taken down to the station and held in a cell all night long. In the morning, they took us back to the bar and made us arrange to pay for the busted window.

I remember another time some of the guys bought counterfeit $20 bills from this guy that was in the funny money business. They'd get Jergen's lotion and smear it all over the bills, and then lay the bills on the radiator to soften them up. They'd take them to Coney Island or someplace like that, and buy something for a dollar, and get $19 back in good money. That was pretty stupid, because the guy who sold them the bills got caught and went to jail. Luckily my friends got away. Nobody snitched anybody out. No goomba ever would.

That's because if you're really friends with a guy, you share everything—your money, your food, your car, your girlfriend, whatever. And when there's trouble, you share that, too. For example, I had this thing happen to me in Vegas.

I was working as a bouncer in this club. One night, this Asian guy got out of line. He was drunk and I had to throw him out. Later that night, he comes back—but now he's got twenty-five friends. They're Chinese, and they're part of some Chinese gang. They come in one at a time, quietly. Before I know it, there's twenty-five of them, and they're looking for me. The good news is they're all about five feet tall. The bad news is they're all black belts. Soon we're in the parking lot, and it's a horrible mess. I'm on the ground. I'm getting kicked in the head. I'm bleeding. I'm taking a beating. All the other bouncers and all the valet parking guys are fighting these Chinese guys. Finally, they've had enough and they take off.

But we think they're coming back. Word gets out, and I start getting calls from everyone I know. They're asking me, "What do you need? What can I do?"

And one guy, this guy I know from the old neighborhood, has a plan. There was a billboard right outside the club. This guy wants to climb up onto the billboard, with a rifle, and shoot anyone who comes after me.

I thought the guy was joking. It's insane! It's murder! He wasn't joking. He said, "I'll pick 'em off for you." He was ready to go.

It didn't come to that, and it was a terrible idea, but that's one measure of goomba friendship. What you find out is your real friends are the guys you can call when things get really bad—when you're in jail, someone is hurting you, or when, God forbid, someone is hurting your family. That's when the real friend steps up and says, "Tell me what you need. I'll do anything you ask me."

And that's how you find out what kind of friend *you* are too. You find out because people call you at three in the morning and say, "Come to me. I need you. I need help now." That's how you know someone thinks of you as a real friend.

On the other hand, there's certain lines you can't cross, even with a best friend. There's certain things that can ruin a goomba friendship. Here are some of them.

Things a goomba will never say to a buddy:

"I'm sorry I can't come to your wedding. I've got Mets tickets."

"We should get matching bathing suits for the beach this summer."

"A hooker for your bachelor party? That's disgusting!"

Some topics are off limits, even with your close friends. The goomba is not going to talk about sex with his girlfriend, even with his best buddies. He might talk about a girl he's dated, but never his girlfriend. He'll point out some girl in a nightclub and say, "I was with her last night," and then give a blow-by-blow account of the whole evening. But he won't say anything about his girlfriend.

That would be disrespectful, for one thing. And for another, the goomba does not want his friends imagining him in bed with his girl. You don't want your friends to have a mental image of your girlfriend that way. It would almost be like if they went to bed with her themselves. So, the goomba doesn't talk much about that.

On the other hand, the goomba will help a friend get laid without even thinking about it. You introduce each other to girls you know. You tell girls about this friend of yours, how great he is, what a great guy he is. Sometimes the goomba will dump a girl he's been seeing, a girl he's not serious about, but then introduce her to a friend who he thinks will like her. There's no shame about such things, between friends.

Goomba guys do lots of stuff together. But there are certain activities that are off-limits. If you want to have goomba friendships, you have to learn to behave in an appropriate manner. It's not as simple as it looks. A goomba guy will cook dinner and serve it to the guys, for example. This is considered manly behavior. On the other hand, goomba guys never sit side by side in a restaurant booth or hold hands when they're walking down the street. That's pretty obvious. But there's other stuff that isn't so obvious. Here are some examples.

Things goomba friends can do together:
- Go to a ball game
- Go to a pool hall
- Go to a bar
- Go out for Chinese food
- Go out for any food
- Share a pizza
- Share a hooker

Things goomba friends *can't* do together:
- Dance
- Take a yoga class
- Shop for lingerie—for themselves
- Get their nails done
- Visit a massage parlor where they actually give massages

Those goomba friendships from childhood last a long time. I know guys now that I knew in kindergarten. We're still best friends. And I have friends whose fathers are still friends with guys *they* knew in kindergarten. They've been friends for sixty or seventy years. There are still some things that the closest friends would never say to each other. You wouldn't want to criticize certain things, no matter if the guy is your best friend in the world.

Things the goomba never says to a pal:
"You bought a Cadillac? What are you—gay?"
"I tasted your mother's meatballs. Disgusting!"
"The New York Giants? What a bunch of retards."
"Tony Bennett sings like a fruitcake."

The friendships keep the neighborhood alive. My friend Mike grew up in Canarsie. Him and his brother Frank. Their dad worked as a cashier on Wall Street. Mike was at home, on his sixteenth birthday, fooling around on the living room sofa with this girl he was dating. It was the middle of the day. His dad came through the front door. Mike said, "What are you doing home in the middle of the day?" His dad said, "They let me go."

Mike thought they gave his dad the day off. He was happy for him. He went back to fooling around with his girl. That night, he found out his dad had been fired.

They didn't have any money. They were broke. The guys in the neighborhood heard about this problem, right away, and they found him work. The wiseguys in the neighborhood particularly took up the slack. Pretty soon Mike's dad has a job tending bar at the wiseguy social club. He's got a job delivering bread for a bakery the wiseguys use. The men on the block found things for him to do, so his family would have enough to eat.

I remember Mike's dad had a stroke, when Mike was around that same age. His dad's best friend was this ironworker named Tommy Thompson. He was like another father to Mike and his brother. While Mike's dad was in the hospital, Tommy would come home from work every day, get cleaned up, and take Mike to visit his dad. And the whole way he'd tell him stories about his dad. He said, of all the men he had ever known, his dad was the only one he'd consider if he needed a guy to watch his back. Here's this big tough ironworker, telling Mike that his laid-off cashier dad was the only guy he could ever depend on.

That's a real goomba friend.

Later on, I found out what a great friend Mike was, too. A real goomba friend.

I was newly married. My wife and I didn't have kids yet. She was working as a cocktail waitress, at the same place Mike was working. And every two or three days, she'd come home crying. There were these two manager-type guys who were just killing her. Criticizing her. Giving her trouble. She'd come home crying, wanting to quit, mad at these guys but not knowing what to do about it.

I knew what to do about it, believe me. But what I wanted to do was not the right thing to do—unless I wanted her fired and me in jail. So I called Mike.

I said, "You know these two guys, right? They're breaking my wife's balls. You gotta make them stop. Because if I come down there, I'm gonna hurt somebody bad."

Mike knew I was serious. We'd been through some stuff together. He knew that if this stuff with my wife didn't stop and I had to come down there, somebody was going to the hospital.

So he went to the two guys. He said, "You know this Laura? You gotta back off with her. She's married, and her husband is not happy with the way she's being treated around here, and he's not a guy you want to mess with."

The guys said, "What the hell does that mean? Are you threatening us?"

Mike said, "No. But you guys know where I come from. You know the kind of people I know. If you don't want to start having to watch your back, I'm telling you, you got to lay off this girl."

It stopped. Right then. Over. I never even had to go down there. Mike said, "I think I took care of that thing with your wife."

He could have been fired. He could have been arrested. He could have been killed, for all I know. But he didn't care. I was his friend. I had a problem. He made it his problem, and he took care of it.

> Long story short, when times are tough, there's no better friend than a goomba. Here's some other ways you can tell if your friend is a true goomba.
>
> ### YOUR FRIEND ISN'T A GOOMBA IF:
> He owns a smoking jacket.
> He thinks Cadillacs are just for black guys.
> He says things like, "Sure! I'd love to tell you about my business!"
> He says things like, "Why Italian? Why can't we go out for weiner schnitzel?"
> He says things like, "Have you heard the new Waylon Jennings CD?"

The goomba always looks out for the fellow goomba. When I was a young goomba, newly arrived in Las Vegas, I had no money. I was working and trying to get ahead, but I was broke all the time. Luckily I had some fellow goombas looking out for me.

One guy, for instance, used to bring in these groups of Chinese gamblers. He'd book them into this one particular hotel. They'd all get penthouse rooms, they'd have these entourages of people with them, and they'd stay for a week—gambling, drinking, dining, going to shows, the whole deal.

This friend would call me and a couple of other guys. He'd tell us that Mr. Hong Wang was staying in Room 2220. He'd tell us to go see Johnny Rico in the hotel coffee shop. So we'd all head over there and eat a huge meal—prime rib, steaks, shrimp cocktail, the works! We'd get Johnny Rico to bring us the check, and we'd sign it off to Mr. Wang in Room 2220.

We'd do this all week. From Monday to Saturday we'd eat like kings. Then Hong Wang would go back to Hong Kong, and we'd go back to starving.

There was another guy named Joey that lived with me and some other guys. Joey had an uncle who was a high roller. He liked to stay at the Dunes. He'd come out from Brooklyn several times a year, and all the guys at the Dunes knew him well.

Every once in a while, the uncle would call the Dunes and say, "My nephew Joey wants to come in for dinner with some friends. Will you take care of him for me?" And that's all it took. Joey and me and some other guys would go to the Dunes, to the fancy restaurant there called the Dome of the Sea. We didn't have enough money for a tip at a place like that. We didn't even have the right clothes. The maitre d' would have to get a couple of sports coats for us even to go in the place. We'd scrape up between us a few bucks for the maitre d', and then we'd sit down and eat. We'd have lobster, and bottles of Mumms and Moët & Chandon. We'd eat like millionaires. The meal was all comped—because that's how high rollers like Joey's uncle got treated in those days.

And that's how Joey, being a good goomba, looked out for his goomba friends.

The guys in the neighborhood shared everything with each other. You'd borrow toys, cars, tools, clothes, and even girls. Since nobody had much, everybody understood sharing. If you had to go to a fancy party or something, you'd borrow a suit. If you were broke, you'd borrow a sawbuck. And if you were horny, you'd borrow a girl.

Not a girlfriend. Nobody fooled around with anyone else's girlfriend. That was sacred. If your friend was going out with a girl, and he was serious about her, it didn't matter how you felt about her—

she was off limits. Not only could you not touch her, you had to make sure nobody *else* touched her either. If you saw her out with somebody else, you'd go break it up.

In fact, this was so true that most guys wouldn't date someone's *ex*-girlfriend, either. Or someone's ex-wife. Among the neighborhood guys, if this girl was with so-and-so, then she was taken. If they broke up, she was . . . used. She'd have to find someone from another neighborhood, or someone who wasn't friends with her ex-boyfriend or her ex-husband. The guys in that immediate circle wouldn't go with her.

GOOMBA PERSONAL ADS

AGE: 39. No, 40.

OCCUPATION: I'm in cement.

LAST GREAT BOOK I READ: *Pastafazool for the Soul.*

FAVORITE ON-SCREEN SEX SCENE: The scene in *The Godfather* where Sonny is banging that girl against the door at his sister's wedding. I had sex at a wedding like that one time. Unfortunately, it was my wedding.

BEST LIE I EVER TOLD: What, after this?

IN MY BEDROOM YOU'LL FIND: Come and have a look, baby!

IF I COULD BE ANYWHERE RIGHT NOW: In a cheap motel room with you and a pizza.

On the other hand, some guys would share hookers. A bunch of them would get together, pool their money, send one guy to negotiate with the hooker, and make a deal—eight guys for a hundred bucks, six guys for fifty bucks, whatever. They would line up and take turns. The guy that did the negotiating got to go first. I don't know how they decided who had to go last. Probably the littlest guy, or the youngest guy. Or the dumbest guy.

In fact, I heard a story about a group of guys who were always pooling their money to get a hooker, but who were always so broke that they could never raise enough to actually get the hooker. So one guy volunteered to take the bankroll to the track. He'd play the horses and win until he had enough for them all to get a really high-class whore to do their bidding.

Guess what? The guy lost. Or, that's what he said, anyway. Nobody got laid that day. Except, probably, the guy that went to the track. He probably did just fine.

Some guys I knew used to go into Manhattan to a whorehouse on 46th Street. One guy told me that when he was about 16 or 17, he and some friends would get together and go into the city. There was a door you had to knock on. You went inside, and there was a teller. You'd pay the teller—it was ten bucks for a "half-and-half," which was a blow job and then straight sex—and you'd get a little ticket. Then you get buzzed into this waiting area that looks like a doctor's office or a dentist's office. Outside, it looked like Stalag 17. There were these two Doberman pinschers guarding the cashier. But inside, it was a little waiting room. You'd sit and the girls would come out and sort of walk around while you made your choice.

Even if you saw one you liked, right away, you couldn't do anything. You had to wait awhile to make sure you saw them all. The goomba doesn't want to jump the gun. The goomba wants to make the right choice. So you'd wait until all six or seven or eight of the house girls had finished with their business and come out. Then, you make your choice. You go back into a little room. No, not a room. A *cubicle*, like in an insurance agency or something, with walls that didn't even go all the way up to the ceiling. My friend told me you could hear everything going on in the other cubicles, even if you couldn't see. You'd give the girl your ticket to show you paid, and bingo! There you were. If you wanted to go around again, you could get that for an extra $5.

If you're doing okay, and a goomba pal is down on his luck, you do what you can to help. I could tell a thousand stories about this—about one goomba helping another. Most of them are just about one guy giving another guy a couple of bucks to tide him over. Some of them are more creative than that.

My friend Joe, when he left New York and moved to L.A., was really down on his luck. He kept taking restaurant jobs and kept getting fired, usually because he knew more about cooking than the chef did and refused to cook things the wrong way. Whatever, he wound up broke all the time.

A friend of his was this screenwriter. He knew Joe was having a hard time, so he started inviting him to the movies. It was the end of the year, which means all the movies that might qualify for an Academy Award are playing in the movie theaters. If you're a member of a Hollywood guild, like the Writers Guild or the Screen Actors Guild or the Directors Guild, you get to see most of these movies for free. You just show your Guild card, and you get a free ticket.

Joe's a smart guy. One day he asks his friend, "Can I borrow your card? I want to go to the movies tomorrow."

Being a good goomba pal, the guy says, "Sure," and forks over the card.

But Joe doesn't go to the movies. Joe goes to Kinko's. He makes a beautiful copy of the guy's guild card.

Then he starts making money with it. Every morning, all through the month of December, he goes to the movie theater and uses the card to get a free ticket for the 6:00 show or the 8:00 show or the 10:00 show. Then he comes back a little later, and goes to a different ticket window, and does it again. He does this several times. By the middle of the day, he's got eight or ten or twelve free tickets to that night's shows.

That night, he comes back. He makes a big noise about how long the line is. He pretends to be looking for his friends. He makes a big noise about not being able to find them. Then he turns to someone waiting on line and says, "I already got two tickets. But I'm not waiting in that line to get in. Tell you what, I'll give you the tickets—half price." Within fifteen minutes or so, Joe has sold the twelve tickets he grabbed earlier in the day. By nine o'clock, he's raised $40 to $60.

So, being a good goomba, what does he do? He calls some girl he's been trying to date, and asks her out. And he takes her to dinner. And a movie! Using the same card he copied off his buddy.

When his buddy found out about the scam, he wasn't even mad. He laughed. He thought it was a good scam.

The friendship thing can cut both ways. This is something I've only found out recently, since *The Sopranos* got big and people started recognizing me. I've become a sort of celebrity. People have started treating me different.

I hear from people now that I never used to hear from. I hear from people I hardly know. Most of them don't want anything from me, except my time. Most of them want to hang out.

I had a call recently from a guy I've known for twenty years. He's not a friend. He's not even an acquaintance. He's just a guy I've seen around. He called me out of the blue and said why didn't we get together for dinner.

I said, "Thanks, but I don't think I can. I got the show, and I'm working on a new book, and I'm doing this TV thing."

And he said, "Oh, I see. Mr. Big Shot Hollywood doesn't even have time for dinner anymore?"

Now, this is a guy I hardly know. I don't think he's ever called me before in his life. I said to him, "I've known you for twenty years. Did you ever once ask me to dinner before? Why are you asking me for dinner now?"

These days I get calls from guys who used to snub me. I see guys that never had two seconds to talk to me before, and now they act like we're old buddies.

I hate to sound cynical, but I've got this feeling they wouldn't be acting that way if I was working at McDonald's. Call it a hunch. I don't think they'd be calling if I was mowing lawns.

Guys ask me to come to parties now. They ask me to come meet their cousin Louie. They ask me to come to their cousin Louie's restaurant. When I get there, there's fifteen people I've never seen before, and they all want my autograph. Or I get there and I find out it's opening night for the restaurant, and I'm the "celebrity" they've invited to make it look like something special.

It's weird. People think you're somebody new just because you're on television. At book signings, or at personal appearances, I've had people ask me to sign autographs because they think it will help them with their love life.

I had a guy say to me recently, "Make it out to Mary. If you sign it and say something personal, I know I'm gonna get laid tonight."

I said, "Wait a minute, pal. You're going to use my picture to get *laid?* What's in it for me?"

Another guy asked me if I could sign an autograph for his girl-friend and then meet her personally. It was very important to him. He said, "If you do that for me, I know she's going to agree to marry me."

I said, "I sense a red flag here. If this is the way you're going to get her to marry you, you got problems ahead."

It's like that joke I heard about Don Rickles. Years ago, he was at the Riviera, having dinner with this girl he was crazy about. She wasn't so crazy about him. Rickles saw Frank Sinatra across the room. When the girl got up to go to the ladies room, Don snuck over to Frank. He said, "Excuse me, Mr. Sinatra. I'm sitting over there with this girl. I'm nuts for her, but she thinks I'm a loser. If you could just pass by the table on your way out, and just wave and say, 'Hey, Don,' it would really impress her. She might not think I'm such a bum."

Sinatra, being a great guy, agrees. When he's leaving, he stops by the table. He puts his arm around Don's shoulder and says, "Don! How ya been, pal?"

And Rickles looks up, all annoyed, and says, "Fuck off, Frank. Can't you see I'm busy?"

People start behaving strangely to you when you're famous. I have had three guys call me in the last month and ask me for money. These are not guys I know all that well. One guy called and said could he see me about a problem he was having. I agreed to meet with him. He said he was having financial trouble. Having trouble making ends meet. He said, "I need you to lend me some money."

I said, "I don't know if I can help. What do you need?"

He said, "I need to borrow $50,000."

People think, if you're on television, you're rich. Like I've got $50,000 laying around the house. Is this guy nuts?

On the other hand, and this is kind of sad, I've got friends who don't call anymore. I don't hear from them. Or I hear that they've had some kind of party or something, and I wasn't invited. Or, worse, they're having some kind of trouble and they didn't call to ask for my help. Then I bump into them someplace. I say, "Where have you been? Why didn't you call?"

And they say, "Aw, I figured you're busy all the time now. I didn't want to bother you."

"Bother me? You're one of my oldest friends!"

"I know. But I see you on TV with the show and all, and I figured you don't have time . . ."

Just to set the record straight, I'm still the same guy I was when I was bouncing drunks out of nightclubs, and I'm still the same guy I was when I was booking comedians into the Riviera, and I'm still the same guy I was working as a maitre d' at a big casino when I couldn't get cast as the guy playing the maitre d' in the film *Casino.* Nothing has changed.

People may think I'm out every night hanging with big movie stars, with no time for my old friends. That's the Hollywood way. But it ain't the goomba way.

Over the last couple of years, because of the success of *The Sopranos* and my first book, *A Goomba's Guide to Life,* I get recognized when I go out. And I get treated special, too, when I go out. Someone's always trying to give me something free—a free drink, a free dessert, whatever—and offering to get me into the V.I.P. area.

I was out with John Ventimiglia, who plays Artie Bucco on *The Sopranos* and who's a good friend of mine. He's been a New York actor forever. So he gets invited to these New York actor parties. We were at this thing recently, and someone grabbed us and led us to the V.I.P. room. It was roped off and the regular people couldn't go in there. Ooooh. The roped-off section!

When we got inside, there were all these big-time, talented actors. They're sitting on couches, almost talking to each other, smoking cigarettes. So we sit down. I don't smoke cigarettes. Someone passes me a joint. I don't smoke marijuana, either. So, we just sit there, on the couches, looking at each other, looking at these actors looking at each other. This is the V.I.P. room?

I told John, "I'll see you later. I'm going back out with the human beings."

This happens a lot when I go out with *The Sopranos* guys. We'll

Tony Sirico: A goomba on top of the world with friends.

be at some bar or club and we'll get pushed over into the V.I.P. section. And what's in there? A bunch of other actors and celebrities, sitting around, so cool and exclusive that they've got nothing to say. We're so exclusive that we're all alone with each other.

My wife and I were in a club recently, drinking at the bar. The owner came over and pulled us away. He wanted us to sit in this roped-off "celebrity" area. For what? If I wanted to be alone, I would have stayed in my hotel room. When I go out, I want to go *out*, and be around people. Regular people. Real people. I'm around enough celebrities. When I'm not working, I want to be a regular guy among the regular guys.

When I'm around a bunch of

My pal Dominic with friends at his bachelor party.

stars, I don't know what to talk about with them anyway. The whole cast goes out to Beverly Hills once or twice a year, for the Screen Actors Guild awards and the Emmys. We stay at the Peninsula Hotel. We go to the ceremony together. You stand around with cocktails for a while before the actual event begins. I never know what to say to anybody. I've got all my friends there from the show and sometimes they have their husbands or wives with them.

(In 2003, in fact, for the first time, I attended the event with my oldest daughter. We stayed together at the Peninsula. She got her hair done at the salon there, and she got a manicure and a pedicure, and we walked down the red carpet together. It's the most fun I ever had at the SAG awards, to tell you the truth.)

Other than that, I see all these famous people standing around and I don't know what I'm supposed to talk about with them. "Oh, Halle Berry. I really enjoy your work." I mean, what are you going to say?

But sometimes, I have to admit, I bump into someone I really admire. Sometimes someone will say something really nice about *The Sopranos,* about my work on the show, and I get a kick out of that if it's someone whose work I respect. I have to admit I enjoy it, because I never think anybody even knows who I am.

Joe, Louie, and Carl were three of the closest friends I ever had. Joe Mascali. Louie Modafieri. Carl Bini. I knew these three guys almost my whole life. I went to kindergarten with Carl. I went to grammar school with Louie. I know Joe from the neighborhood. I was at Joe's wedding and Carl's wedding. Later on, when they got married, I knew their wives, too. I went to grammar school with Carl's wife Christine. I went to high school with Louie's wife Joanne. I got to be friendly with Joey's wife Laurie after they got married. And when they had kids, I got to know all their kids. They got to know mine, too. My daughters called them Uncle Joe, Uncle Carl, and Uncle Louie.

I went on spring break with these guys. I went to Florida and the Jersey shore with them. We hung out on the street corner. We had adventures. We chased girls and got into trouble with the cops and did all the crazy things that goomba kids do.

Then we grew up. I moved out to Las Vegas. They stayed in the East. All three of them became firemen and moved to Staten Island. They stayed real close, the three of them, but I kind of lost touch. I was doing my thing, trying to make a life for myself in

The Village People on the boardwalk in Jersey.

Las Vegas. They were living in Staten Island, working hard for their families, building their careers, making a go of it.

Then, out of nowhere, in January of 1999, I get a call. Joey and Carl are coming to Las Vegas, for Super Bowl weekend. They want to get together. I was working at the Riviera at that time, so I told them to come to the hotel when they got in.

When I saw the two of them coming across the hotel lobby, I swear it was like twenty years disappeared. Like I had seen them yesterday. It's just like twenty years never happened. I take them out that night, and we have a lot of laughs. We eat and drink and I get them into a couple of shows. They had a ball. Remember, these guys were firemen. They were real middle-class, hardworking, 9-to-5 guys. They were very domesticated goombas. So this was wild for them.

I really did it up for them. When they ordered room service, I had the chef himself go to their room to serve them personally.

Little did I know they were going to return the favor. Six months later I got asked to come to New York to audition for this new TV show called *The Sopranos*. Carl picked me up at the airport. Joey drove me to the studio for the audition. He even waited for me, in the car, while I did the audition. When it was over, we went to Sheepshead Bay for baked clams and fried calamari.

I got the part, and I started coming back to New York regularly. Every time, either Carl or Joey would pick me up at the airport. I'd come in on the redeye flight, and they'd pick me up at 5:30 in the morning, and take me to wherever I was staying.

Later, when I became a regular on the series, they moved me to Staten Island. They helped me find a place. Then, because I was in Vancouver working in a movie, they took care of my wife and children until I got there. They unloaded the moving van. They moved Laura into the place. Later, when we moved back to Las Vegas and I needed an apartment in Manhattan, these guys moved all my stuff into my new apartment and got it all set up. I wasn't even there. They just took care of it.

Once I was spending time in New York on a regular basis I saw these guys all the time. I'd take them to *The Sopranos* premieres and introduce them to the guys in the cast. We'd go drinking. We'd eat in the best places. Several times people would see us and mistake Carl for John Ventimiglia, who plays Artie Bucco. They'd want to take our pictures and get our photographs. There's a lot of pictures out there starring Carl as Artie Bucco.

I really tried to show them a good time. And we had so much fun together. Lots and lots and lots of laughs—just like when we were kids.

These guys did everything for me. They did for me like I've never done for anybody. There was nothing they wouldn't take care of. When my car broke down, Louie was there.

One time I got an early morning call from *The Sopranos* studio. Some actor was suddenly unavailable to work that morning. I wasn't scheduled to come in until noon. Could I come in right then? I said I could. Then I called Joey. He arrived, in a fire truck. He hit the lights and the siren and I swear we made it from Staten Island to the studio in Queens in forty minutes. All *The Sopranos* people were freaking out. They said, "How the hell did you get the fire department to drive you here?" I said, "Hey, you said you wanted me here in a hurry. I got here in a hurry. Don't ask how."

I don't know how they made time for me. They were all incredibly hardworking guys. Louie had just taken the test to be a battalion chief, and passed. But he also had a car repair business on the side. Carl had been a fireman forever, but he also had a cabinet-making business. Now he and Joe, even though they were still firemen, also had a construction business on the side. (For Joe, this was the family business. His father was in construction. In fact, it was his father that ran the chimney sweeping company that I worked for when I was a kid.) It was nothing for these two guys to make a four-hour drive to some construction site in Connecticut, work all day and then make the four-hour drive back.

These guys were tough, but they had huge hearts. These were real goombas. Super-goombas. You know what firemen are like to begin with—there's nothing they won't do for someone in trouble. These guys were like that off the job, too. Joey was always helping people out with money. He once gave me enough money to go to Florida on spring break. He picked up many a tab back home, too.

On the morning of September 11, 2001, all three of them were working in Staten Island, in the firehouse, where they were known as Rescue 5. That morning Rescue 5 went into the World Trade Center. The building collapsed. Joey, Carl, and Louie never came out.

The news killed me. It just killed me. It tore my heart out. I didn't leave the house for three days. I never knew I could cry that much.

Later, I went to their memorials. Three separate memorials. To

Great goomba friends reunite in the neighborhood.

see the agony of their families was horrible. Each memorial service was harder than the other. Then Christine asked me to speak at Carl's service. It was the hardest thing I ever did.

What's incredible to me now is how their wives and families have held up. All three of them were married to these wonderful goomba-ettes—smart, beautiful, tough girls who are still in there, still working hard, still keeping their families together. It's very inspiring to me to see how strong they are, how strong they stayed after what happened. It's a real testament to these goombas that they chose such strong, wonderful women.

Even now, not a day goes by that I don't think of these guys. I remember something we did together, something one of them said, and I get torn up all over again. But I also feel very lucky to have known them. They taught me everything I know about goomba friendship.

Looking for Love:
The Goomba's Guide
to Dating

The goomba guy,
he'll date anything.
He just wants sex.
Unless he's starting
to get serious.
Then he won't be
serious about a girl
who'll give him sex.

*Y*our average goomba is a guy who takes his loving seriously. He's gonna get laid, one way or another. If it's not this girl, it's another one. The goomba is persistent. He ain't going home alone.

But he's not a moron. He knows how to treat a lady. He knows how to keep certain things to himself. There are some things you won't catch him saying out loud.

Things a goomba will never say to his girlfriend:
"Gina, I'd like you to meet my wife."
"Of course you can date other guys."
"I think that dress is cut too short."
"A blow job? No thanks. Maybe another time."
"Me, you and another girl? That's sick!"
"Let me pleasure *you* tonight, honey."

When we were teenagers, my friends and I talked about sex all the time. Sex and sports, but especially sex. We'd talk about girls we were interested in, girls we thought were cute. We'd look at a girl walking through the neighborhood, and say, "Jeez, that's a nice piece of *bracciole.*" A *bracciole* is an Italian dish, kind of a spiced meat dish, where you slice the beef real thin and then roll it up with cheese and stuff inside. To call a girl a nice piece of *bracciole* was a high compliment in my group.

If a girl was really pretty, she was "the nuts." If she was super pretty, she was "the stone cold nuts."

We talked about wanting sex a lot. We used the "F" word a lot, but more as a general curse word. When we talked about sex, we had special lingo.

Someone would talk about dating a particular girl. The holy grail was "in there." When a goomba would go on a date, his friends would say, "Did you get in there?" Or he'd be talking about how beautiful she was, and he'd say, "Jeez, I'd love to get in there."

Another expression was "get over." We'd say, "How'd you do? Did you get over?" Or a guy would say, "I'd sure like to get over on her."

Body parts had special goomba nicknames, too. A girl's breasts were knockers or knobs. We knew a guy named Dobbs who was going out with this girl with really big breasts. We'd say, "There goes Dobbs, with the knobs."

The vagina was the "twatzone," pronounced like it was Italian, a new word that took the idea of "calzone" and put sex in it.

When we were younger, we'd stand around the street corner and check out the girls going by. We'd give some of them a hard time— especially if they were older and good-looking. We'd wait for a pretty girl to pass, and call out, "Hey, cookie!" When she turned, we'd say, "Not you—you crumb." Or we'd call out, "Hey, dream-boat!" When she turned, we'd say, "Not you—you shipwreck."

We'd see a pretty girl in the street, and say, "You know what would look good on you? Me!"

By the time we were teenagers, we were getting even more stupid. We'd ask girls, "Do you like sausage?" or "Do you like to eat sausage?" We'd say, "Did you ever have sausage in the can?" Most of the time the girls didn't know what we were talking about. We'd practically fall over from laughing, and they didn't even know what we were talking about.

A guy that was very successful with the girls, or who had a reputation for being fast with the girls, he was a "stick man." A guy that was getting a lot of sex, he was a "plow boy." We'd joke about "plowing," like we were a bunch of farm boys from the country.

However, when we were out with girls, we all acted like big men. We'd try to treat the girls like our fathers treated our mothers. Some guys would get mad if their girls used rough language. "Don't curse," they'd say. Some guys would get mad if their girls got too dressed up. "You look like a *puttana*," they'd say. "Go change that dress."

If we were in a club, some guys would tell their girls, "I want to see you staring straight ahead. You don't even *look* at another guy."

RESPECT

One thing I notice is different on the East Coast and the West Coast. If you go into a restaurant on the East Coast, with a beautiful girl on your arm, all the guys will turn and look, once, and then they'll turn away. If one of them keeps staring, someone will say, "Hey, show some respect. She's with him."

On the West Coast, and in Las Vegas, forget it. You walk into a club with a good-looking girl on your arm, the guys will turn, and look, and keep looking. You get up to go to the bathroom, they'll actually come to your table and try to hit on the girl while you're gone.

Guys that try that where I grew up are going to wind up with their heads kicked in. In Las Vegas, I see it all the time.

We were very territorial about our girls, too. If a girl from our street went to a club and met some guy and brought him back, we'd give him the cold shoulder. He wasn't from our neighborhood. He was no good. We'd give the girl a hard time, too. "So the guys from around here aren't good enough for you—that you have to go and pick up some guy from someplace else?"

But we were protective of the girls, too. We'd say, "If that guy touches you, you let me know." Like we were their fathers. Like we weren't touching them ourselves!

Some of the girls took that crap. They'd get all meek and say, "Okay." Other girls, they didn't want to be treated that way. They'd say, "Enough of that greaseball shit. You're not my father."

Of course at that time it was mostly talk. Some goombas, to be perfectly honest, are a little messed up about sex. They come from old-world families. Maybe they come from very religious families. Maybe they have a mother who's deeply religious and obsessed with the evils of sex. The goomba can be ruined for life by this.

My friend David, from Astoria, told me about how he and some guys conspired to get their friend Michael laid for the first time.

He was about 20 or something, and he was still a virgin. David knew this girl who was kind of loose. She was actually living in a spare room in his place. So he said to her, "I got this friend who's a virgin. He's a nice guy. Would you mind, you know, showing him the ropes?" She said she didn't mind.

But David knew Michael wouldn't go for it if he just told him, "There's this broad upstairs dying to go to bed with you." He knew he had to trick him. So he told the girl to put on something sexy and wait until this guy Michael showed up, and then seduce him.

Then David called Michael and a couple of other guys. He told them he had this huge kitchen table that he had to get out of the apartment. He lived on the fourth floor of a building without an elevator, so he was going to need help. Naturally all the guys agreed.

They met on the street in front of the apartment. David gave Michael the keys. He told him, "You go up first and get the door open. We'll get things ready down here and be right up to join you."

Michael takes the keys and goes up to the fourth floor. The other guys go across the street to look up at the window. They figure once Michael gets into the apartment and sees this broad in the sexy lingerie, he's going straight into the bedroom.

They wait, and they wait. They don't see anything. They're staring at the upstairs windows. They figure Michael's in the saddle already. Success! Another satisfied customer!

Then one of the guys says, "Look! It's him!" and points to the front door of the building.

Here comes Michael, huffing and puffing, carrying this huge kitchen table on his back. He hits the street and dumps the table down on the sidewalk. David and the other guys rush over. Michael says, "You tried to trick me!" and storms off.

Upstairs, the girl tells David, "That friend of yours is nuts. He came in, took one look at me, and suddenly started moving the furniture around!"

GOOMBA PERSONAL ADS

AGE: Mind your own fucking business.

OCCUPATION: What are you, nuts?

LAST GREAT BOOK I READ: The Racing Form.

FAVORITE ON-SCREEN SEX SCENE: Now we're getting someplace. When Mickey Rourke eats the food off Kim Basinger in *9½ Weeks*. That's entertainment.

BEST LIE I EVER TOLD: When I told the judge, "So help me God."

IN MY BEDROOM YOU'LL FIND: Some broad.

CELEBRITY I MOST RESEMBLE: Alec Baldwin, but a little . . . heavier.

I moved out to Las Vegas when I was a young goomba. I had already had a few girlfriends, in high school and college. I had fooled around plenty. Let's just say I knew my way around the female form.

I'm not sure exactly *how* I knew what I knew. I never got the birds-and-bees speech from my father. I certainly didn't get it from my mother. By the time I was in Health class, I already knew what was what. I picked it up the same place I learned everything else— on the corner, on the block, from the guys.

There was a local guy who was our pharmacist. We called him "Doc." One day when I was about 15 or 16, I ran into him on the street. I said, "Hey, Doc! I got a question. What's the best thing to use for a contraceptive—to not get a girl pregnant?"

He pulled his glasses down over his nose and looked at me and said, "The tongue, son. Use the tongue."

Those were his words of wisdom. Some advice.

There was another guy in our neighborhood named Pete. He was our baseball coach. Very good guy. Very dedicated. He was single and still living with his mother, and he was about 35. I was maybe 16. Pete would give me and the boys lessons about love and sex. He was full of useful advice. For example, one day he told us boys what to do if you want to go with a hooker.

He said, "Remember this, boys. When you go with a hooker, always jack off first. You hear me? You jack off before you go. That way, when you're with the hooker, it will last longer. You'll really get your money's worth."

Then he told us this didn't always work out. He said he was with a hooker once. He had jacked off first, of course. And he's with her and he's having a wonderful time, just going and going and going. After an hour, he's still going. And she says, "That's it, pal. You're done." He had used up all his time.

He would tell us stories about getting laid, too. We'd be driving in his car, to a baseball game, and he'd say, "You see that seat? Right where you're sitting? I was with a girl in the car last night. She was screaming and yelling. 'Give me more! Give me more!' I told her, 'That's all I got! I don't got no more!' "

I don't remember when I discovered sex, exactly. It was just something you knew about. It was something the older guys talked about, or made jokes about. I do remember there was a drugstore in the neighborhood, and that pharmacist would show "French" movies in his basement. They were black-and-white movies, in French. But that was pretty hot stuff.

Somehow you would always hear about some girls in the neighborhood who were willing to fool around. One time, when I was 16 or so, these friends of mine told me and my buddy about these two girls they had met. They'd picked them up on the corner, on 82nd Street in Bensonhurst. They weren't hookers. They just liked to fool around. These guys told us they'd picked 'em up and had sex with them.

We said, "Get outta here!" But we went up there to check it out. We took my friend's dad's car—a big goomba Cadillac Eldorado. And there they were. They were just girls who liked to fool around. We took 'em out, took 'em for a ride and . . . baboom! There we were. I was in the back seat with one girl, and my buddy was in the front seat with the other girl.

Goomba-ettes in Brooklyn, 1977.

My first kiss—I was about 11. The girl's name was Cindy. I rode over to her on my bike and asked her if she wanted to go out. She said, "Sure." So I rode back to where my buddies were waiting to find out what she'd say, and I told them she said yes. Then I rode back over and gave her a kiss. I think I scared her. She let me walk her home and kiss her again, but then she ran inside.

On graduation day, at the end of the sixth grade, we all went to the place called Jahn's for ice cream. It was like this fancy diner that served ice cream sundaes. After that, we went to the movies. It was like a big date. I went out with Cindy all summer. Then we broke up.

A couple of years later, I was maybe 14, and this friend of mine—Joey Animal, they called him—had a party. He was 16. It was the first party I ever went to where there was alcohol. This guy's dad was the bartender. I had a couple of beers. And there was this girl there. She was 14, too. We went outside together and started to make out. I was feeling pretty bold, so I decided to take a chance. I put my hand under her shirt. She let me! First time for that. We were out on the side of this house, in the yard, lying in the gravel, right there on the ground. Very romantic. I loved it!

Later, in high school, I lost my virginity with a girl we called "I Love Lucy." She had red hair and a big mouth—she was no oil painting, but she was willing. And I was horny. I took her for a walk, and we ended up down by the golf course, which is where you took a girl if you wanted to fool around. It was in the middle of the summer, and hot, and sticky. By the time it was over, I had so many mosquito bites on my ass that I could hardly sit down, but I wasn't a virgin anymore. I thought it was all going to be easy after that. Getting sex was going to be like picking oranges in California—you just reach out and . . . bingo!

But it didn't turn out that way. I discovered that getting laid was hard work. Sometimes, you'd turn to a professional for help. Some of the guys went with hookers.

Mostly, though, I tried to get dates with attractive goomba-ettes from the neighborhood. The most beautiful girl I ever tried to go out with was named Annette. When I asked her if she wanted to go out with me, she said, "Sure, Stevie. If you were the last fuckin' human being on the planet." I was devastated. I later heard that she married this guy named Artie, who became a butcher, and that she started putting on the pounds. Now she's got an ass the size of Rhode Island. Serves her right.

Unfortunately I did not know then what I know now. If I could go back to high school, knowing what I know today, I'd be getting laid seven nights of the week. But in those days I didn't understand girls, or dating, or sex, or anything. There was no one around to teach me. My dad wasn't around, and I didn't have a helpful older brother or cousin or uncle to take me under his wing and say, "Here's the deal, kid . . ." So I had to make it up as I went along.

Now, I know how it's done. I learned by trial and plenty of error so you won't have to, so you can take this stuff to the bank. Here's just a few pointers to get you started.

Things a goomba should not say on a first date:

"Relationship? No thanks. I'm just interested in sex."

"I'm planning on spending a lot of money tonight, but I expect to get laid before it's over."

"Actually, both my parents are in prison."

"Sure I've got a sister. How else would I learn to kiss like that?"

Things a goomba should not do on a first date:

Tell her how much time you spend thinking about sex—especially sex with *her*.

Tell her how much money you make—or don't make.

Tell her how much money you intend to spend on her.

Tell her how much sex you expect in return.

I lost my virginity when I was barely 16. After that, I had sex with every girl that would say yes. Why not? I was young. It was the 1970s. Sex was not as dangerous then as it is now. I did a lot of dating.

I had a lot of sex, too.

A lot of time we'd have to leave the neighborhood to get sex. For spring break all the guys would go down to Florida. During the summer, we'd go down to the Jersey shore. It was a huge group of us—twenty-five or thirty guys—and we'd fly down, or take the train, and get rooms in a hotel. We'd go to Fort Lauderdale, or Wildwood, and we'd go nuts. It was nothing but drinking and sex. For most of the guys, this is where the goomba learned about love.

We'd spend the day by the pool, drinking beer, getting a suntan, and making moves on the girls. When you found one that was interested, you'd go out for a meal. Pretty soon, if it's clicking, you're in the sack. There's no time for dating. The girl was

Goombas in Fort Lauderdale with $300 between them.

probably there with her family. She might be there for two or three days, tops. So everything had to happen fast. You fall in love with a girl, and you're together with her exclusively. But two days later, she's gone, and you're with another girl. Over the course of a three-week vacation, I might be with ten different girls. And I loved them all—for a while.

The same was true for my friends. We always did extremely well on these vacations. It was like that movie *Where the Boys Are,* but with more sex. Someone's doing it on the beach. Someone's doing it on the lifeguard tower. Someone's doing it in the broom closet. Someone's doing it on the bed. Someone else is doing it on the other bed. Someone's on the couch. Someone's in the parking lot. Someone got a key for an empty room, and two or three guys are with their girlfriends in there.

And no one was safe. We were doing it with the girls, with the girls' mothers, with the maids, with the waitresses. Anyone! Everyone! The goombas went wild.

Remember, these are all guys who are 17, 18, 19 years old. They all still live at home. Most of them have got girlfriends, but they're goomba girlfriends and they're living at home, so what are you going to do? Where are you going to go? You can't stay up all night having sex with the girl back home. And you can't go to a hotel without her parents and your parents knowing something's going on. It's impossible.

Down in Fort Lauderdale, no one's watching. You can do anything you want. So, you do *everything* you want.

We had all kinds of pickup lines. Some of them were pretty crude, but that's the goomba way. There's no point in beating around the bush. The goomba wants to find out, right away, if the girl is interested. If she's not, *fugheddaboudit.*

GOOMBA PICKUP LINES

"Would you like a bite of pepperoni?"

"Can I borrow a quarter to call my wife and tell her I won't be coming home tonight?"

"Can I buy you a drink? Can I buy you a house?"

"Do you know the difference between a blow job and a baloney sandwich? No? How about lunch tomorrow?"

"Do you have a little Italian in you? Would you like some?"

In the old days, some of the players had their holiday moves down perfect. My pal Charles Najjar, one of the great old-time goombas, used to go down to Florida for his vacations. The first day there, he'd go down to the pool and hook up with the pool manager. He'd duke the guy $20—which in the old days was a fair piece of change—and tell him, "Every time I come down by the pool, I want you to set me up next to the most beautiful girls down here. Don't wait for me to ask where I want to sit. Just get me set up next to the most beautiful girls." That way, every day, he found himself within striking distance of the best girls.

He had another trick that was also terrific. He used to date a lot of stewardesses and they were always really good-looking girls. Charles knew these girls didn't make much money, so they always roomed in groups of four or five and they never went out for expensive meals. Whenever he'd meet a stewardess, he'd ask her on a date. Whether she was anything special or not, he'd take her out for a very fancy evening—drinks, dinner, expensive wine, the works. She'd go back and tell all her roommates that she met this great guy.

The next time Charles called the girl on the phone, if she wasn't there, he'd say, "She's not home? Who's this?" Then he'd identify himself. The roommate always knew who he was—that great high roller!—and nine times out of ten she'd agree to go on a date with him, too. Sometimes he'd make it with the first stewardess he took out. Sometimes it would be one of the roommates. More often than not, it would be more than one of the roommates. It was like having a harem.

A goomba on spring break.

Those days were gone by the time we got to Florida. So sometimes we'd get carried away. One time at the Jersey shore we caused so much trouble that the police were called. They literally made us pack our bags and followed us in their police cars until we were over the county line.

Another time, the motel manager found out we had broken some furniture. He came to the room and started telling us how much he was going to charge us—so much for this chair, so much for that chair, so much for this table . . . So one of the guys says, "I gotta pay for all this? Then I can do what I want with it!" He busted up the rest of the furniture and started hurling it off the balcony, from the third floor, down into the parking lot. (That wasn't a motel we went back to.)

Another time, we were going nuts and throwing people into the pool. It started with us throwing each other in. Then we started throwing the girls in. Then it was other people we didn't even know. Then it was the hotel staff. It ended when we chased this maid around the pool. She was yelling, and we were laughing and teasing her. But then someone threw her in. Unfortunately, she couldn't swim. She sank to the bottom like a rock. The goombas panicked. We were sure we were going to jail for murder. So we ran.

Turned out she was okay. But it was still a crappy thing to do.

We were young and stupid. We did stupid stuff. One time we all went to Hawaii on the same kind of trip. But a couple of the guys were not having any luck. They had done good in Florida and on the Jersey shore, but in Hawaii they couldn't get laid. So finally they decided to go with a hooker. After they were with the hooker, one of them realized his wallet had been stolen. They went back, but the hooker was gone. So the next night, two guys went back to the hooker's apartment. They took everything she owned—her clothes, her furniture, her plates and glasses—and paid her back by throwing everything into a dumpster.

Most of the time we never saw the girls again, after the spring break or after the summer. We planned to. We'd exchange addresses and we'd write, or we'd promise to write. But it never came to anything, or nothing good, anyway.

One time we met these girls from Montreal in Florida. They were beautiful, and really nice, and really rich. We didn't have any money. I mean, I'd go to Fort Lauderdale for spring break for three weeks with only $150 to my name. I'd stay as long as I could, and leave when the money was gone.

These girls didn't care if we were broke. They had plenty of money. Every night, they were taking us out for drinks, taking us for dinner, taking us everywhere. I remember one of them, at a restaurant, ordered a bottle of wine that cost $20. We couldn't believe it—what class! We thought we were on easy street. It was like we were gigolos or something. We were used to Gallo Hearty Burgundy, wine that was $5 a gallon.

After the summer, they came to New York to visit us. They stayed at the Waldorf-Astoria. The Waldorf-Astoria! We had sex with rich girls in the Waldorf-Astoria.

Then they invited us to come to Montreal, as their guests. They told us to drive up and check into this hotel. They said they'd take care of everything, because they knew we didn't have any money. So five or six of us packed into the car and away we went. Now we were traveling gigolos. We had visions of this mansion the girls lived in. We thought our ship had really come in. We were set.

Bear in mind, we were not in love. I didn't even particularly like the girl I was with. She was okay, but it wasn't any big thing. I knew she was very enamored of me. But I was not that enamored of her. I just loved the idea of going with a rich girl.

We got to Montreal and found the hotel. We got on the phone. And the girls were not there. We got one of their mothers on the phone. She told us the girl was not there, and wasn't going to be there. The girls had stiffed us!

We were pissed off. We wanted to know what the hell had happened. We had been writing letters, so we had a couple of addresses for these rich bitches. We got into a cab and headed out for the rich part of town where these girls lived in their mansion.

The joke was on us. We found the first address. It was a crummy little run-down house in a working-class neighborhood. No mansion. We went to another address. Same thing, right around the corner. Another crappy little house.

The goombas had been duped. We went back to the hotel with our tails between our legs. We didn't have enough money to even pay for the one night, let alone the seven nights we had been planning on. We scraped together our cash and got one guy to use his parents' credit card. One of the girls finally called with some bullshit story about her father getting sick or something. We stayed two days and then drove home. It was a long drive home.

Another time these girls from Chicago that we'd met in Florida came and stayed in Brooklyn. The minute they arrived, we knew we didn't want them there. We started trying to figure out how to get rid of them. My buddy went through one girl's purse when she wasn't looking. He found a letter in it. It said, "Don't forget, the minute you get back, come up to my place, and sit on my face. Love, Stan." We thought: "Those whores!" It was over.

Back in the neighborhood, I was more careful about the girls I went with. You want to be a little selective. So when you meet a girl, you check her out. If she goes to your school, or lives in your neighborhood, you probably know what you need to know already. You know her family, or her brothers, or her cousins, or her friends—or probably all of those people.

But if it's a girl from a different school, the goomba's gotta do his homework. He's going to ask around. He's going to find out who she knows, who she hangs out with, who she used to go out with. If she went out with some jerk, he needs to know that. If she's got a bad reputation, he needs to know that, too. The goomba doesn't want to go walking down the block and have everyone laugh at him—'cause they know she's a *puttana*.

And pity the poor goomba who doesn't do his homework. My friend Mike almost walked into a world of pain one time because he wasn't paying attention.

He was working at a restaurant when they hired this new girl. She was young and innocent-looking and incredibly beautiful. Mike befriended her—because of course he wanted a taste of that. She told him she was sad because her boyfriend was mean to her and didn't let her go out. She didn't know anyone. She never went anywhere. So Mike, being the gentleman he is, invited her to come along with him and a group of people who were going out that night to some club.

That night, things were going great. Everyone was drinking and

GOOMBA DATING TIPS

Do ask her if you can pull out her chair.

Don't ask her to pull your finger.

Do tell her you've got "protection."

Don't tell her that means you're paying a mob guy not to burn down your place of business.

Do write her a romantic love poem.

Don't begin the poem with, "There once was a man from Nantucket . . ."

Do compliment her on her new outfit.

Don't say, "It's tight on you, but I like a girl with a fat ass."

Do take her to meet your mother and father.

Don't do this until they've been released from prison.

Do take her to a nice place where everybody knows your name.

Don't take her to Big Ed's Live Nude Girls, even if that's the only place where everybody knows your name.

Do take her to a sexy movie, like *Chicago*.

Don't say, "Jeez, what an ass!" every time Catherine Zeta-Jones comes on screen.

dancing. Mike and this girl were dancing together. She was coming on to him pretty strong. He thought he had a good shot at her. Until someone said to him, "You know who that is, right? You know whose girlfriend that is?"

Her boyfriend was one of the worst of the worst of the worst gangsters of all. Of course Mike knew who the guy was. Mike knew he'd kill *him,* for sure, if he knew Mike was hanging out with his girl. Mike shoulda done some homework.

The goomba guy, he'll date anything. He just wants sex. Unless he's starting to get serious. Then he won't be serious about a girl who'll give him sex.

That's the double standard in the goomba world. The goomba wants to get laid, as soon as possible and as often as possible. But he's not going to settle down with a girl who'll go to bed with him right away. The goomba will never marry a girl who sleeps with him on the first date. Automatically, he knows she's no good. He can never take her seriously as wife material. He might like her. He might even like her a lot. But he can't trust her. He thinks, "If she's sleeping with me, she's sleeping with everybody."

I remember when I was young and single, but starting to think about getting serious, I would go on a date with a really nice girl and I'd think, "Please, don't sleep with me tonight. Not on the first date." Of course I wanted them to, but at the same time I didn't. It's just I wanted to meet someone I could be with in a serious way.

It wasn't just me. I have a friend who had a huge crush on this girl from the neighborhood all through high school. He couldn't even talk to her, he was so in love with her. After high school he moved away. Then he came back. He got a date with her. They went out, had a few drinks, had some dinner, and went back to her place. He couldn't believe his luck. All his dreams were coming true. They were fooling around on the couch when suddenly she unzips his pants and starts to go down on him!

He couldn't take it. This girl, this perfect girl, this girl he had fantasized about for years, she was a *puttana*. It broke his heart. It's crazy, but it's true.

Once the goomba has decided to go to bed with a girl, of course he's got to find a way to get her there. There are lots of romantic things he can do. And there are all kinds of strategies, too. Here are some goomba techniques for getting a girl into the sack.

WAYS TO GET A GIRL INTO BED

♥ Push her onto the sheets while she's making the bed.
♥ Serve her a pitcher of Bellinis and four slices of rum cake.
♥ Tell her, "We have to go to the mattresses."
♥ Tell her, "On my mother's eyes, I won't touch you."
♥ Tell her, "Sleep with me, or you'll sleep with the fishes!"

In the old days, maybe the goomba could insist on marrying a virgin. These days, forget it. No one thinks about that. But the goomba still wants to get as close to that as possible. The goomba doesn't want some hors d'oeuvre that's been passed around already. He doesn't want some cocktail frank.

That's one reason the goomba is going to check the girl out. It's one reason he's going to keep his mouth shut about his girl, too.

One goomba I know, he went out with this girl who did him on the first night. She was wild in bed. The next day, he told his friends about it. He gave them a blow-by-blow account of the whole night. She did this, and she did that, and then she did the other thing.

But then he went out with the girl again, and he started to like her. He went out with her some more, and he started to like her a lot. Then he fell in love. Pretty soon he was engaged to marry her. And he's already told all his friends she's a complete freak in bed. The real goomba, unless he's a moron, he doesn't do that. He won't tell his friends what his girl does with him in bed. In fact, he'll go the other way. He'll *lie* about what they do, just to make sure no one gets the wrong impression of his girl. He'll say, "A blow job? No way. My girlfriend don't do that. We might have kids one day. She's going to kiss her children with that mouth!"

Other stuff, other positions, you don't tell your friends about that either. If you're dating a girl who likes it doggie style, you would never talk about that. That stuff is for freaks and porno stars—not for nice girls. The goomba may love it, but he keeps it to himself.

*True Love: The
Goomba Relationship*

If you ask most goomba guys what they're looking for in a girl, they all say the same thing: "I want someone who's like a girl from the neighborhood."

*I*t usually doesn't take a goomba long to find that one special person, someone he can see having a future with, settling down, having a few kids. Marriage doesn't necessarily mean forever—or even that he stops looking for that special someone *else*. But marriage is always part of the picture.

For example, this friend of mine called me once and said he needed my help. He said, "I got married, and I don't wanna be married."

I said, "You're telling me *now?* I coulda been your best man!"

"It was sudden," he says. "I got married at 4:30 this morning. And now I want out."

He tells me he met this hooker. She was off duty. The meter wasn't running. He wanted to take her home. She said, "I don't go with guys that don't pay me unless I'm married to them."

So he said, "Then let's get married!"

Off they go. Now he wants out. So he needs a lawyer, and he needs to get an annulment. He married her, and he got to sleep with her for free. So, he saved $200. But the annulment ended up costing him $1,000. So he was out $800. He shoulda just paid her a couple *hundge* up front and done it the old-fashioned way.

That wouldn't have been love. But it wouldn't have been as expensive either.

For most goombas, love is a sacred thing. Maybe goombas don't experience love differently from other people, but they take it seriously. For example, look at the movie *Titanic*. To most people, this is one of the greatest love stories of all time—right up there with *Romeo and Juliet*. To the goomba, it's not a love story at all. To my friend Frankie, it's a disgrace.

As he points out, *Titanic* is the story of this poor girl who pretends to be rich so she can get on the boat and marry this rich guy and live happily ever after. But instead she meets this poor guy. She falls in love with him, and goes to bed with him, and then steals some jewelry, and then the boat sinks. The guy she loves dies. She lives to be about a hundred years old.

To Frankie, this is an outrage. First of all, he says, no self-respecting girl would pretend to be rich just to marry a rich guy. "She's a *whoo-ah*, right from the start," Frank says. "She's this low-life, white-trash broad, trying to pass, trying to get some guy for his money. Her mother is trying to help her sell her virginity to a rich guy! Instead, she meets another low-life. *She shtups him,* right away. In a car! They're on the fanciest boat in the history of the world, and she *shtups* him in a car. Only a slut does that.

"Then she steals the rich guy's jewels. So she's a thief, too. Then the boat sinks. She's floating around in the water with the man she supposedly loves. Does she say, 'Let me get in the water with you'? Does she say, 'You float for a minute while I swim'? No. She watches the guy turn white and sink and drown.

"Then, a hundred years later, she's living with her granddaughter or her niece or something, and she's so old she can't wipe her own ass. Does she tell the niece, 'Let's sell the jewel so we can hire a nurse to wipe my ass'? No! She keeps the jewel to herself and lets her niece keep suffering. Then, when she's going to die, she throws the jewel in the ocean so nobody can ever have it but her.

"What a bitch!"

Frankie points out that a goomba girl would never do any of that. First of all, no self-respecting goomba girl would ever go with a guy just for the money. And no goomba mother would ever help her daughter become a whore like that. To the goomba, there is no difference between the prostitute who's giving blow jobs for twenty bucks and the girl who marries a rich guy for twenty million. If it's not for love, she's a whore.

Second, a nice goomba girl ain't going to bed on the first date. With the goomba girl, you ain't getting laid for at least three months. Any girl that goes on the first night, she's a *whoo-ah.* Especially if it's in the back of a car. The goomba girl, if she's on the Titanic, she's going to insist on a nice room, according to Frankie.

But this girl is a tramp. Not only does she sleep with the guy, right away. Then she takes her clothes off and lets him draw pictures of her. What a pervert! She's into porno, basically.

Third, a goomba girl doesn't pretend to be something she isn't. She's not going to try and pass for a rich girl. She's going to say, "I may not have much, but my family brought me up right and I'm a good cook and I will stay by your side forever. My love outweighs any riches you could ever have."

Fourth, the goomba girl is not going to let her man suffer without trying to do something about it. She's in the water, the goomba-ette, swimming right along with the guy.

And last, the goomba girl ain't greedy. If she's got the jewel, she's going to fence it and take the money and spread it around. She certainly isn't going to keep her niece around to wipe her ass when they could hire a nurse to do that.

To the non-goomba, though, this is a great love story. Go figure.

If you ask most goomba guys what they're looking for in a girl, they all say the same thing: "I want someone who's like a girl from the neighborhood. I want someone who's like from back home." It doesn't matter where the guy lives or how old he is or how far away he is from Queens or Staten Island or Bensonhurst. They want a girl who's like a girl from the neighborhood.

When they meet a girl they like, they say, "She's just like back home." In fact, unless they *are* from back home, they are *never* like from back home. But that's the goomba ideal in a way. What they really mean is they want someone who acts like their mother and has sex like a hooker. She is great in bed, but cooks sauce on Sundays.

This is the classic goomba girl. First of all, she's good looking. Got to be good looking. The goomba ain't dating no dogs. She's dark-haired, of course. (You don't find too many natural blonde

Goomba-ettes at a wedding in Vegas.

goomba girls.) She's got to have a good body, too, and she's probably going to show it off—tight pants, tight tops, all that. But she isn't going to be flaunting. The goomba doesn't want a girl who looks like a whore. Just a girl who's great looking and knows it. She's going to be a good dancer. She likes getting dressed up and going out.

She's not going to be covered in tattoos, or have pieces of metal stuck through her nose, or have spiked purple hair. The goomba ain't bringing that home to Mom. The goomba takes one look at a girl like that, and he can already hear his mother saying, "Not for nothing, but she looks like a fishing lure." The goomba might like the idea of a girl with a spike through her tongue, but if she clicks every time she says hello—no.

She's also going to have a rough mouth and a pretty nasty accent. The goomba doesn't want one of these mousy, thin-lipped

WASPy blondes. The goomba wants a broad who's just as loud as he is. He wants a girl who can smoke and drink and take care of herself and have a good time.

You go to any club in Jersey, you can see these girls. They travel in packs. Groups of five or six of them will come into a place and grab a table and start ordering drinks. And then a group of five or six goombas will come in and start looking them over and pretty soon it is *on*, baby. That's goomba love.

When I was coming up, girls were pretty conservative, especially girls from the neighborhood. The goomba-ette, she's not giving anything away. She may be wearing tight pants, but just try to get inside them! In those days, you might take a girl out three or four times before you even got a kiss. Another month, you might get to fool around a little. Another six months, you might get to have sex. A girl might sleep with her boyfriend, but it happened slow. None of this jumping in the sack for the goomba-ette. They don't want to get a reputation.

No, the guy on the left is not wearing a costume.

They don't want to start people talking. Remember, these girls are from neighborhoods where everybody knows everybody. Everybody knows everybody else's parents and grandparents. A girl that's sleeping around, pretty soon everybody's going to know about it. So those goomba-ettes were careful about what they did.

It starts very early, that stuff. My friend Mike was in the sixth grade. It was Valentine's Day. He had a girl he was sort of going steady with. Her name was Louanne. He gave her a Valentine's Day card. But he also gave Valentine's Day cards to two other girls that he kind of liked.

During the lunch break, everyone was exchanging their cards. Mike felt a tap on his shoulder. He turned around. Louanne slapped him on the face so hard that he almost fell down. She said, "Don't you *ever* cheat on me!"

It became known as the Valentine's Day Massacre. The whole school talked about it for weeks. We were 11 years old.

Guys who grew up in the neighborhood eventually got around to dating, and most of them dated Italian girls who lived down the block or around the corner. When I left the neighborhood and went to Las Vegas, I couldn't believe how different the girls were. Guys would go out on a first date and wind up in bed. On the first date! Unbelievable. Some guys I knew, they thought they'd died and gone to heaven. They were getting laid every night!

GOOMBA DATING 101

This is the kind of wisdom they would have been given, if anyone had taken the trouble to write it down.

Do bring her 12 red roses.

Don't bring a 12-pack of Bud.

Do take her to a night club.

Don't take her to a strip club.

Do steal a kiss.

Don't steal her purse.

Do open the car door for her.

Don't open the trunk for her.

Do use the proper cutlery while dining.

Don't wipe down the silverware when you're done.

My friend David, for example, told me a story about when he first came out from Astoria, New York, to Las Vegas. He got a job in a casino. He started flirting with this change girl. By the end of the shift, he'd made a date with her. They go out for a few drinks and then they're back at his place. Pretty soon, she's got his pants off and she's giving him a blow job! He's ecstatic, naturally, but he also wants to make love. She seems like she doesn't want to. But he keeps trying. Finally he says to her, "Look, this is incredible, but I really want to make love to you." She looks horrified. She says, "Are you kidding? I don't even *know* you!"

But here's the weird part. Ask them what they're looking for in a girl, and those goombas would still say they wanted to meet someone who was like the girls back home, girls from the neighborhood. They loved all the sex-crazed broads they were meeting in Las Vegas, but they still wanted to marry a girl from the neighborhood—a nice girl, like their mother.

The same thing is true with the goomba girls, too—but even more so. The goomba-ette will go on vacation to Florida or someplace, and she'll meet some guy from another state and start dating him. Every single time, he's another goomba. He might be from Chicago or South Philly or whatever, but he's the same kind of goomba the girl dates at home.

Some guys, though, even before they leave the neighborhood, they go outside the neighborhood, and date non-goomba girls. That can break your balls, too.

When I was young, I went out for a while with this Jewish girl. Smart. Beautiful. Not a goomba-ette in any way. In those days I wasn't looking for a goomba girl. I liked the way they looked, but once they'd open their mouths—forget it! It's over. I couldn't be around a girl that talked like me.

The trouble with this girl is her father hates me. Absolutely hates me. He's the father of a nice Jewish girl from Sheepshead Bay, and I'm not good enough. Now, I'm half a Jew myself. He knows that, but he forgets that. He doesn't see a nice guy, taking his daughter out, treating her good. He sees a guy who's not acceptable, because he's not Jewish. When I'd go over there, the guy won't even speak to me. One time, my name was in the *New York Times,* because of the basketball team I was on. The girl shows her father, and he's got nothing to say. He just stares at me. All because I'm not Jewish.

So, the beginning of the end: Someone had given me a beautiful piece of jewelry. A cross. I show up to take my girl out, and she sees it, and she says, "You can't wear that in the house. My father won't allow that."

That was it. Over. We broke up. I really felt bad. She moved to California. I moved to Vegas.

The funny thing about it is this: When my mother married my father, his family wouldn't accept her because she was Jewish. In fact, the day before they got married, the priest came to my father's house and tried to talk him out of getting married. His family didn't want the marriage to go through. I think one of them put the priest up to making the call. My mother was never really accepted by my father's family. And here I am, a young goomba, getting a taste of the same thing, in reverse. This girl's father won't accept me because I'm *not* Jewish.

The knife cuts both ways, too. A goomba friend of mine was in love with this Jewish girl. Her parents were wealthy, and they didn't trust the guy. Plus they didn't want their daughter to marry anyone who wasn't Jewish. They tried like crazy to bust the thing up, and it worked. The girl dropped my friend, and pretty soon he found out she was marrying this other guy—a Jewish guy that she didn't love. She was doing it to please her parents. Well, a year later, her parents were both killed in a car crash. She was stuck, married to this guy she didn't love. My friend ended up marrying a nice girl from the neighborhood. And the girl that married the Jewish guy ended up divorced.

Which is why most goombas are gonna end up with a goomba girl sooner or later, one way or another.

The dating part is not that complicated. But there are special rules for goomba dating.

For one thing, goomba girls are conservative. I remember one time when I was young there was this new girl who moved into the neighborhood. Pretty soon she's hanging out with the other goomba girls. She's in one of those packs of goomba-ettes. And this one night, in a club, she fools around a little too much. She starts making out with this one guy, on the dance floor. And an hour later, she's dancing with a different guy, and she's making out with him.

Goomba-ettes: They look tougher than the guys I know.

That don't go. The other goomba girls, they sit this girl down and they tell her, "We don't do that. We are not whores. We don't mess around with two guys in the same night. You do that, you're going to get us all a bad reputation."

Even the girls who go for sex in a big way are worried about their reputations. I have this friend who started dating this girl. They started sleeping together, and she gets wilder and wilder in bed. She likes it this way and that way. She likes to talk dirty. She likes it when he talks dirty. Like, really nasty.

One night, they're going at it. She says, "Do it! Give it to me harder!"

And he says, "Take it all, you dirty *whoo-ah.*"

That stops her dead in her tracks. She turns and looks at him.

She says, "Did you just call me a *whore?*"

Before he can answer, she's up and out of bed and getting dressed. She's got her clothes on, and she's gone.

And to tell the truth some goomba guys don't want a girl who's too sexual. That can be a big turnoff. If the goomba is in bed with his girl and she starts doing something a little wild, the first question he's going to ask himself is, "Where did she learn that?" He starts wondering who taught her. He knows it wasn't *him*. So, who? He starts thinking, "I got a *puttana* on my hands here." So he's probably going to ask the girl how many guys she's been with. He might ask her what she did with them. And once he starts asking those questions, the end is near. No matter what she says, his imagination is going to start working. Pretty soon, every time they go out in public, he's looking at every single guy and wondering, "Is he one of them? Did she go with him?" If they go to the movies, he starts thinking every guy in the place got there before he did.

Some girls can also be very jealous. You have to watch out for that type. They can be pretty tough. You start dating one goomba girl, and you go out with a different goomba girl, and you see the first girl—watch out! Somebody's gonna get hurt. The goomba-ette can be a very jealous person.

For example, I know this one guy. He and these two friends of his were all seeing girls on the side. They had steady girls, but they had these other girls. They'd see their regular girlfriends on Friday night, but on Saturday they'd go with these other girls.

One Saturday night, they had the girls up in one of the guy's apartments. Two of the guys were in the two bedrooms, banging away. My friend, he's going at it in the hallway, standing up.

The regular girlfriends, they knew something was up. They came to the apartment, and starting yelling and pounding on the door.

Trouble is, this friend of mine is practically deaf. He's standing in the hallway, going at it, and two feet away his girlfriend is pounding on the door and screaming, but he doesn't hear anything. He's got his pants around his ankles and he's banging away for all he's worth.

Boom! The goomba-ette kicks the door in. She sees her boyfriend hammering away at this other girl. She starts yelling and hitting him on the head.

And I swear he says, "Stop! It's not what you think! She's my cousin!"

I don't know why he thought that was going to calm his girl-friend down. But that's what he said: "She's my cousin." Like, that's better?

In the end, a goomba wants a good loyal woman he can marry and spend his life with. This girl, she's gonna do anything for her man. She'll go to the wall for the man she loves. She'd do anything for him, and anything to protect him. I have one friend who's been married a long time. He and his wife have had their ups and downs, believe me. They've been through thick and thin. They've been this close to divorce, a couple of times. But ask him about his wife, and he'll say, "Her? She'd go to the chair for me."

You meet one of those—you're fixed for life. Unless you screw it up. That almost happened to a friend of mine. He was with this girl for a while. One weekend, he went over to a buddy's house. The buddy was out of town, but he had told my friend he could stop by and use the pool if he wanted. So the guy takes his girlfriend over for a swim. They've got their towels and stuff. They've even brought lunch—a big bucket of Kentucky Fried Chicken. They're having a nice afternoon.

Then my friend's stomach starts to rumble. He's got to go. Like, right this second. And there's no place to go. The house is locked. There's no one home. There's nothing nearby, either. They're out in the suburbs. There's no gas station down the block. My friend starts freaking out. He's afraid he's going to let go, right there, in front of his girl.

Well, she notices that something is going on. She asks the guy what it is. And he blurts it out. He's got to take a dump so bad he's dying.

The girls takes the bucket of Kentucky Fried Chicken, dumps the chicken out of it, and hands it to the guy. She says, "Go behind the bushes. Use this."

That's a real goomba broad. Steadfast. Resourceful. Loyal. Not fazed by anything. She's the one that thought of the bucket! A girl like that is like gold. They kept dating and they moved in together.

But some goombas are hard to satisfy. I have one friend who's kind of nutty about how girls look. He's a very successful guy in Las Vegas—successful in his business, and very successful with the ladies. He only dates the top of the top. *Playboy* material. *Penthouse* material. He's single, and he's good looking, and he takes his pick of the best.

And he goes slowly. He'll take a girl out two or three times before he tries to go to bed with her. Because he's so picky. He's got to be sure she's someone he's going to like. So, he's looking for the things he *doesn't* like.

For example, her feet. She's got to have nice feet. Maybe the first date, she doesn't wear shoes where he can see her toes. So, he's going to go out with her again because he's not sure about the feet. If she's got ugly feet—big feet, or big toes, or toes that cross over each other, or toes that hang off the sides of her shoes—he's finished. He won't go to bed with her.

You'd be surprised how many goombas have things like this—little fetishes and little things that turn them off.

I know one guy, if the girl's apartment isn't spotless, it's over.

I know another guy, he was dating this girl. He was falling for her. She was beautiful and sweet. Unbelievable body. Really sexy.

They had been on a few dates. Now it's back to the apartment. They're in bed. They're fooling around. He's so excited he's about to die. She excuses herself to go to the bathroom. He's lying in bed, dreaming about what he's going to do to this girl, when all of a sudden from the bathroom, he hears her fart.

He gets out of bed and puts his clothes on. When the girl comes out of the bathroom, he's on his way to the door. Over.

I asked him what happened with her, and he told me the story. He said, "After that, I couldn't even look at her. How could she fart? How could she do that?"

The fart was the dealbreaker.

There are some general rules for dating goomba girls. If you make a date, you got to keep the date. For you it may be only dinner and a show, but for her—she's already had her hair done, and she's got a new outfit, and maybe she's bought new shoes. You break the date, she's gonna break your balls.

There are also general rules around communicating with your goomba-ette because even in the little things, you have to be considerate. You have to learn to let the girl have the last word on certain things. Make her feel like you are concerned about *her* needs and feelings:

If she says, "That Pamela Anderson looks like a whore," you say, "She certainly does."

If she says, "What do you mean, *Cats* is sold out?" You say, "I swear to God, all Ticketmaster had left was two tickets for the fights."

On the other hand, you have to be firm. If she says, "Not tonight, honey. I feel like I need my space," you say, "I'll rent you a storage garage. Now take off your dress."

Sometimes, it's just the way the girl acts. My friend Charles took this girl out one time. Beautiful girl. Not too bright, and very young, but beautiful. He took her to a fancy restaurant. She asked him, kind of shy like, if she could order the lobster. He said, "Whatever you want!" She orders the lobster. When it comes, she looks kind of confused. She says, "There's no tartar sauce." He told her this was the best lobster in town. You'd ruin it with tartar sauce. She says, "But I like tartar sauce." He says, "Sure thing, honey," and gets up from the table. He goes to the captain, and gives him a hundred bucks. He says, "This is for the meal and for you. Take care of the girl." And he left her there. The tartar sauce, that was the dealbreaker.

He told me he saw her later and she wasn't even mad. She said, "I liked the lobster." With the tartar sauce!

With other guys, the dealbreaker is who the girl dated before she dated him. Most goombas, they think a nice Italian broad can't date anybody that's not an Italian guy. Black guys are no good. Chinese guys are no good. Not even a Puerto Rican or a Russian. Maybe an Irish guy. Maybe a Jewish guy. But that's about it. It's not like the goomba is a racist. But he needs to know.

One friend of mine was out with this broad. He was getting pretty interested. And he was starting to wonder whether this girl was ever with any guys that weren't like him. Right then, he sees this Chinese girl across the room. He says to his date, "That's a nice looking woman, that Chinese woman." The girl agrees. So he says, "Would you ever do that? Date a Chinese guy?"

If she says "yes," she's finished. And she said "yes."

Another time, he had been out with this girl a few times. He was getting serious about her. She had been a cheerleader for the Raiders. Now she was a dancer. She's beautiful. Great body. Showgirl body. Pretty. And he really likes her. One night they're in the car, driving to a restaurant. They're talking about football and she says something about dating one of the Raiders. A running back.

Now, the goomba don't know everything there is to know about football, but he knows a little. And he knows there ain't that many white guys who are running backs. So he says, "No kidding. Was it a black guy?"

Of course it was. The relationship ended right there. The goomba made a U-turn and took the girl home and told her good night. Ciao, baby.

At the other end, you got the goomba guy who'll go with anything. My friend Frank is like that. He used to be a nice Italian boy from Canarsie. After twenty years in Las Vegas, though, he's turned into an animal. He has more sex than anyone I ever knew.

At first he was dating cocktail waitresses. I'd say, "How can you go with a girl who's got her ass hanging out of her uniform and flirts with every customer just to get a tip?"

Then he started dating showgirls. I'd say, "How can you go with a girl who dances around with her ass hanging out of her costume in front of hundreds of people?"

Then he started dating strippers. I'd say, "How can you touch a girl who takes her clothes off and dances around naked for money in front of total strangers?"

Then it was hookers. I'd say, "How can you make love to a girl who will sleep with any guy that gives her money? You can't sink any lower than that."

Then he started going with porno actresses. I said, "That's it. You're a pig. You're the top of the heap of pigs. You can't get any more disgusting than a porno actress."

Now he sometimes goes with two porno actresses at a time, or has a porno actress and a hooker together, so I guess I was wrong.

Once the goomba and his girlfriend get serious, they almost act like a married couple. The relationship is very steady. They're not living together—that's a no-no in the goomba world because both of these people are probably still living with their parents. But they're together a lot. They're exclusive. And they almost always go out with other goomba couples. Saturday night, it's four or five goombas and their girlfriends. They'll meet at a bar or a club, they'll go to dinner, they'll go dancing or to see a show. And the following Friday the same five or six couples, give or take, will do it again. This is the goomba social scene.

Privately, some of them are taking it a bit further. At the end of the night, the goomba and his girl might be having a little goomba sex. They're not doing it at home because home is where their parents live. They might be making it in a car. Or they might be sneaking off to a hotel or a motel someplace.

When I was young, back home, there were places the guys knew where you could get a room cheap. You'd go out to the motels near Newark Airport. Maybe a wealthier guy would do it up fancy—go to Manhattan, take his girl to an expensive restaurant, and spend the night at the Sheraton or something. But the average goomba, he can't afford anything like that. It's gonna be dinner and a little sex at a place they rent by the hour.

If things go along this way for a while, and everything looks okay, the goomba is going to meet the goomba-ette's family. And she is going to meet his family. This is a big part of the dating ritual. (If the families don't accept you, there's no future in the relationship.) You're going to be spending a lot of time with this family. After you start going out, you're going to be invited to all the family events, and the girl is going to come to all your family things— the weddings, the baptisms, Christmas, all that. You might even go on vacation together. That's not unusual. The girl's family will invite the boyfriend to come along for the summer holiday. He's going to stay in the hotel, in a room with the girl's brother or something, for a couple of weeks at the seashore. Or they're going to go on a cruise together. I have a friend with two daughters. He just came back from a cruise, with his wife, his two girls, and the two boyfriends.

If it gets past the first couple of dates, and the girl checks out, the goomba mating dance begins. First thing, the goomba is going to give her a gift. And the first gift, always, is the ankle bracelet. If the goomba is 16 or 17, this is a big thing. He gives the girl an ankle bracelet. But she doesn't wear it around the ankle. She wears it around her neck, attached to a chain. When she's got that on, it means she's going steady, she's spoken for.

If you survive the first year of dating, you and your girl might be on your way to becoming serious about each other. You might even be heading for the altar. But beware. As close as you might be, as loving as you might feel . . . she's still a woman. And, unless you're funny that way, *you're* not. So be careful. There are some topics that you and your girlfriend may never be able to discuss. Here are a few forbidden topics:

Things a goomba can never tell his girlfriend:
"When we have sex, you're almost the only woman I don't think about."
"I bet *I'd* look good in silk stockings."
"If it weren't for your cooking, I'd be outta here."

At Christmas, the goomba is going to buy the obligatory name plate. The goomba is going to buy this thing that spells out the girl's name in diamonds. All the girls have them. They're so ugly, they're hip. When I was a teenager, it was mandatory. You bought one that said "Angela" or "Marie" or whatever. Now the girl can show the world she's serious about the guy, and vice versa. This is for real.

Next, it's the pre-engagement ring. This is kind of a nothing ring—no diamond, no stones—but it's a serious symbol. Things are moving along.

TOP: *Matty and Patty:*
Brooklyn to Vegas to
Brooklyn. Still together.
CENTER: *Joey and Irene: Still*
going strong.
BOTTOM: *What a cake!*

TOP: *Charlie and Gussie: Still happy and in love.*
CENTER: *A beautiful couple: Lori and Joe.*
BOTTOM: *John's much happier now that he's a grandad.*

Then, it's the engagement ring and the engagement party. People who didn't grow up in this world, they never heard about an engagement party. In the goomba world, you have to have an engagement party. It's a very special event. It's a way of announcing the engagement, it's a celebration, but most of all it's the beginning of the financial fund for the wedding.

That's because, just like with weddings and funerals, every guest at the engagement party is going to bring the *a boost*. Every guest is going to bring a little envelope with a little cash in it, to help the young couple get their start in life. At the wedding, *a boost* might be two or three hundred dollars. At the engagement party, it's going to be half that. If you would give $300 at the wedding, for the engagement party you're going to throw down a buck and a half.

The engagement party isn't as big as the wedding. It's held in a hall, or a restaurant, but it's less formal. There probably won't be a band, only a DJ. So the *a boost* is going to be smaller, too.

The engagement party starts the planning for the wedding. The research starts right away. The goomba-ette gets a ring on Sunday, on Monday morning she's buying *Bride* magazine and looking for a hall to rent. She's looking at wedding bands and wedding dresses. She's got the green light. She's off and running.

I was still pretty young when I left the neighborhood. I didn't have that engagement party experience myself. I was with plenty of girls. But I was in Las Vegas before I ever fell in love.

When it happened, I knew something different was going on. I met this woman and I fell hard. She was tall and dark and beautiful. I was nuts for her. We started going out. I was serious.

Then she got sick. Five years later, she died. And I was devastated. I couldn't work or eat or sleep. After some time I found a job in Hawaii; I stayed there for eight months.

Later, I came back to Las Vegas. Then I met the girl who changed my life. I met Laura. She was smart and funny and beautiful. I fell in love. We got married. We had two children. I discovered that my broken heart was mended.

This has all taught me a number of things. First of all, it taught me that while a goomba's appetite for love may go up and down a little, his ability to love does not. Once a lover, always a lover. The goomba heart is a large, forgiving organ with a long memory.

My good friends John and Margaret. Still happy after all these years.

It also taught me that it's never too late. I know one old goomba, a friend of mine from New York, who is 72 years old. He still goes out with girls—at his age he gets middle-aged women, but he calls them girls—two or three nights a week. I ask him, "You're 72 years old! What are you gonna do with a girl like that?" He says, "Same thing I always did with them. And keep your voice down!"

All in all, it's amazing the goomba ever gets together with anybody. And this is why so many goombas keep their love life right there in the neighborhood. It's just easier.

That's what happened to my friend Joe Soup—Joe Gannascoli, who runs the soup restaurants.

Joe met Donna in Wildwood when he was about 18. He and a bunch of his friends would go up there every summer, and stay at the Wildwood Crest. They'd go in a group of twelve, and stay four guys in a room, and chase girls all day and night. Donna was a dark-haired beauty from Bay Ridge. Italian. Nice. Same age, but a month younger. They were made for each other. They started getting serious after the summer.

TOP: *Joe and Donna back in the day.*
BOTTOM: *Joe and Donna look as good as ever and even happier.*

But Joe was a dog in those days. He was a real skirt-chaser. Later on, he got a little old, he got a little heavy, time took its toll like it does on all of us. But in those days, he'll tell you, women used to throw mattresses out the window when he walked down the street. And Donna wouldn't stand for it. She wanted a nice boy who was going to get married and settle down and be a father. Joe wasn't ready. Donna bailed out. Later on, she married another guy and moved to Staten Island.

Joe would get reports from time to time. Donna had a kid. Donna had another kid. Donna has three kids. Joe was sowing his wild oats—working in New Orleans, living in Los Angeles, making it as an actor, making it in the restaurant business. Every few years he'd hear something new about Donna. And once in a blue moon he'd see her. Usually she'd needle him about getting older, getting fatter, letting himself go. "You used to be so vain! I can't believe you look like this now," she said to him one time.

Time passes. Joe makes a fortune, loses a fortune and is back in Bay Ridge. It's twenty years later. He and a partner take over this storefront, and turn it into a successful restaurant. It's on the same block where Donna grew up. It's in the same storefront, in fact, where Donna's father used to have his "social club" with the other Italian guys from the neighborhood.

And by now, Donna is divorced. The kids are grown. Donna's watching TV and what does she see? Joe, guest-starring on *The Sopranos*. And love blooms again. Goomba love is back. It's twenty years later, and neither one of them is a kid anymore, but it's goomba love just like that first summer in Wildwood.

Joe said to me recently, "I'm telling you. I still get excited when I see her. To this day, I still have that same feeling as when I first laid eyes on her." That's some goomba love.

*Tough Love: The
Goomba Family Man*

Want to make a goomba tell the truth? Get him to swear on the heads of his children. No real goomba can do that and tell a lie.

*N*othing is more important to the goomba than his family. Bottom line, this is it. *La famiglia!* The family is sacred. Want to make a goomba tell the truth? Get him to swear on the heads of his children. No real goomba can do that and tell a lie. His family means more to him than anything else in his life.

It's also the secret of his masculinity. If you think a tough guy isn't sentimental, you haven't met a real goomba. The real goomba is a family man.

Remember the scene from *The Godfather?* Don Corleone is giving a lecture to Johnny, the singer from California who wants to get into the movies. (I know you remember what happens to the movie studio boss who won't give him a part in the movies, right? He winds up getting a little head—but it's the head of his favorite race horse, stuck beside him in his bed.)

Don Corleone asks Carlo, "Do you spend time with your family?"

"Yes, Godfather."

"Good," Don Corleone says. "A man who doesn't spend time with his family can never be a real man."

There you go. A goomba without a family is like macaroni without sauce. The goomba needs to be a family man. It's his goomba destiny. He wants a big noisy household, filled with kids he can scream at then tell them to stop making so much goddamn noise.

He wants a wife he can come home to—just not always on Friday night, which he might want to spend with the guys, or with the girl-friend.

The goomba wants to be part of a big extended family, too. Most goombas have six or seven cousins that live on the same block as them. Half those guys are named after the same person—the grand-father they all share. So there's four guys named Tony, or four guys named Angelo, or four guys named Anthony. (I was going to be named Ilario, after my grandfather. I don't know what happened with that.) Most goombas have so many cousins, they could call their mechanic, their plumber, their electrician, their accountant, their travel agent, their lawyer, and their bookie and still not speak to anyone they're not related to. They're all cousins!

You can identify the goomba dads in the group from the way they talk. They don't talk like the other fathers.

Things a goomba dad might say to his kids:

"Go down to the corner and tell Tony I want the Jets ten times."

"There's no bugs under your bed. I had Uncle Paulie sweep the room last night."

"One more 'F' on your report card and you're sleeping with the fishes!"

"I'm sorry I missed your Little League game. I had a bail hearing."

"This is going to hurt you more than it hurts me."

Some goombas will do the most incredible things to get a fam-ily. There was a story in the papers recently about a New York mob guy who was in prison since the late 1980s. In the late 1990s, though, the feds get word that he's being visited in prison by his wife and a child—and he's telling everyone it's *his* child! Which is impossible. The kid is about four. The mobster's been in prison ten years, with no visitation. The feds discover the guy has smuggled his sperm out of prison to impregnate his wife! What a goomba! He's a family man, in every sense of the word.

It takes more than a big bunch of kids and a noisy extended family to make a guy a true goomba family man. Think you might qualify? Ask yourself these questions:

♥ Have you ever asked a family member to lie to the police for you?

♥ Have you ever asked a loved one to destroy evidence for you?

♥ Is your wedding day on video—an undercover surveillance video?

♥ Have you seen pictures of your family members—hanging in the post office?

♥ Have you ever received a birthday card, anniversary card, or Father's Day card—while in a correctional facility?

The average goomba will be able to answer "yes" to at least one of these questions. Or, if not, he can certainly say, "No, but I know a guy that happened to." The average non-goomba can't.

The important thing about the goomba family is this: The goomba loves kids. He loves big families. He's gonna get one, if he can.

Or, maybe, more than one.

I used to know a goomba from Chicago who had a terrible father. He wasn't necessarily a bad guy, but he was a bad father. He wasn't around. He was in and out of debt, and in and out of jail. He didn't provide for his family.

This guy had been fooling around behind his wife's back from almost the day they were married. He had this girlfriend he's been seeing almost as long as he's known his wife. And the wife knows about it. The guy promises to break it off, and the wife believes him. But pretty soon she finds out he's still seeing the girlfriend.

It's a rocky marriage. They have kids. But like I said the guy's never around. He's working, or he's hiding from the cops, or he's hiding from his bookie. He's in, he's out, and his family never knows when they're going to see him again.

One night, when my friend is a teenager, this woman shows up at his house. She's drunk, and it's the middle of the night, and the woman is screaming. "He doesn't love you!" she's saying. "He never loved you. He only loves me!" This guy is shocked. He can believe a lot of things about his old man, but he can't believe the guy's got a girlfriend that loves him.

Turns out he has more than that. When his father dies, the son finds out there's a whole second family. Two miles away, halfway across Chicago, living in an apartment just like the one he lives in, his father has a whole second life—a common-law marriage to this crazy girlfriend, and two kids. They're almost as old as my friend! They've even got the same last name.

His mother has known about the relationship the whole time. She tries to forget. She tries to forgive. She has three children with this man, and she's completely dependent on him for support. What's she gonna do?

But when she finds out about the two kids, that's the limit. She refuses to let the family put a death notice in the newspaper announcing that her husband has died. Why? Because she's terrified his second family will show up at the funeral home or the cemetery and shame her.

So these poor other kids, their father has died, and they can't even find out where the funeral is being held. Their father is buried, and they don't even know where.

Years later, my friend met someone who knew the other woman. He had heard his mother talk about her since he was a teenager—

she was a slut, she was a whore, she was a bitch. So he asks this guy, "What was she really like?"

"As nice a woman as you could ever want to meet," the guy says. "A lot like your mother, in fact. A terrific woman."

And that's not even so unusual. I know another guy and the same thing happened. His father was kind of a playboy, very successful, always on the move, always out of town, doing this and doing that. He was a good provider, but he was never around. He never spent time with his family. It turns out that's because he had too many families to spend time with. When he died, his son became executor of his estate. He discovered in his father's papers that he had another wife, and another bunch of kids, living two miles away. And that wife and those children thought *they* were the guy's only family, too.

Of course not all goombas behave this way. Even the bad goombas don't behave this way all the time. Even the bad goombas try to do the right thing for their families.

Remember *GoodFellas?* There's this amazing scene right near the end. Henry Hill, the hero of the story, is in bad shape. The feds are closing in. The family has turned its back on him. His wife knows he's cheating. His girlfriend is threatening to dump him. He's got a drug problem that's killing him. He's getting ready to make one more run—selling some stolen guns, moving a shipment of drugs. He's got his wife and his kids and his little brother at his house. And what is he doing? He's obsessing over his Sunday sauce and meatballs! He's got the dinner going, and he's making sure his brother knows how to stir the sauce for him while he goes to sell the stolen guns. The guy's whole life is about to fall in on his head, and he's worrying about getting dinner on the table for his family. What a goomba!

In the old days, the division of labor in the family was clear—the goomba dad worked and the mother stayed home. No mothers had jobs. They did the shopping and the cooking and hung around the neighborhood. Where I lived, you'd see the moms going out every day. There were shops up and down 86th Street in Bensonhurst, under the El. From 19th Avenue on up to Bay Parkway, it was all shops. The mothers would take the babies and the baby carriages and go up to 86th Street. Some of them would meet and play cards and have coffee. They'd go into the neighborhood to do the shopping. Remember, this was before the day of the supermarket. So they'd stop at the butcher, the fish store, the baker, the grocer . . .

The goomba dad was working. All the guys I knew were blue collar, middle-class working guys. They were cops or mailmen. Plumbers or sanitation workers. A lot of them were longshoremen who worked on the docks. They all had great TVs and stereos. And their kids had new bicycles. It's amazing how much stuff those dock workers were able to snake away from there.

Some of the dads were wiseguys, too. We didn't know what they did, exactly, but we knew what they did. They drove nicer cars than the other dads, and they dressed better. If we saw them in the street, they were very polite and respectful. They'd say, "Here's ten bucks. Go get yourself some lunch." We'd go to the corner candy store and buy everything.

A lot of the fathers had a little extra work on the side. They weren't real wiseguys, but they did little jobs for guys who were wiseguys. They had a little numbers thing, or they did a little shylocking. They'd front a guy a couple hundred bucks if he was a little short on his bills. There were always other people behind it, and ultimately it was all mob money, even if the front guy wasn't a mob guy himself.

And everybody always had a lot of swag. People who didn't have clothing shops would sell leather jackets and dresses and suits and shirts. You could buy a nice suit for fifty bucks. Someone would have pocketbooks. Someone else would have perfume. Some guys

Goombas on a Sunday afternoon.

sold fireworks. Swag! You could buy brand new Converse sneakers or Keds for five bucks.

For recreation, the goomba dad did sports things with his kids. Or with his sons, anyway. There wasn't much going on during the week. The goomba dad is tired. He's worked a long day. He may not have a car—my dad never even had a license—so he's probably left the house real early and taken a bus to work. So when he comes home, the day is pretty much over. He's got the afternoon paper under his arm. He expects dinner on the table when he comes through the door. He's going to get cleaned up, eat his dinner, read his paper, and maybe watch a little TV, and that's it. Thirty minutes of *Bowling for Dollars* and he's out.

In those days it was only the mothers at home in the daytime. The kids went to school, then they had an afterschool program, or they ran in the streets. They came home at five o'clock, around the same time the father came home. Then everyone sat down and had dinner. It was very, very important in most goomba households that everyone have dinner together. I knew some families where there was the worst kinds of insanity going on—abuse, alcohol, you name it. But if the family sat down to dinner together every night at six o'clock, they could pretend they were normal.

In my house, even today, a lot of those old rules are still in place. I work. My wife doesn't work. (She did, until she was halfway through her first pregnancy. Then she stopped, and I convinced her she didn't need to go back if she didn't want to.) I'm out and taking care of business, just like an old-fashioned goomba dad, until the late afternoon. My kids come in from school. We sit down and eat the dinner that my wife has prepared, every single night, at six o'clock.

I'm doing what the classic goomba dad was doing forty years ago. I never planned it that way but maybe I'm just trying to get now what I never got as a kid. No big family meals for us. In fact, I remember my father always being out at night. After dinner, especially if it was a Friday night, he'd get all decked out in the suit and the shiny shoes and the tie and the aftershave. We'd be in our pajamas, all ready for bed, and he's going out. But that doesn't mean he wasn't a goomba dad, or that he never did stuff with us—when he was around.

During the daytime, every weekend, it was baseball. A lot of goomba dads coached their kids' baseball teams. Little League was a big deal in Brooklyn. All the kids played for the church teams. I played for St. Francis Cabrini. Later, I was on the Ty Cobbs. It was very competitive and the dads took it very seriously. When the weather was good, we'd play two or three games every weekend.

If there was no game, the goomba dad was taking his kid to watch the Yankees or the Mets. This was a big, big thing for me. My father might not have done the right thing all the time, but he did take me to ball games. And the movies. We'd go to see every James Bond movie, and sit with our popcorn. It was as close to normal as we ever got.

A lot of the goomba dads spent Sundays working on the car, washing and waxing their car, or working in their gardens. It's amazing to me now, but even the families with the tiniest apartments always had a little garden someplace. The dad would have a fig tree, or he might grow some *gagoots*—that's squash—and he would definitely be growing the things he needed for his Sunday sauce. He'd have tomatoes and basil, at the very least. This was the goomba dad's pride, or the goomba granddad's pride.

But there's all kinds of weekend activities, on the other hand, that you'll never see the goomba dad doing.

The goomba dad ain't golfing. Any guy that owns golf clubs, or *belongs* to a golf club, can't be a real goomba. It may be okay for the Jewish guys or the WASP guys, but the goomba ain't golfing.

The goomba ain't mowing the lawn. First of all, the goomba is a city creature. He doesn't have a lawn. And if he lives in a place where the grass grows like that, he's going to get someone else to cut it. If you have enough money for a garden, you have enough money for a gardener.

The goomba ain't going to no garage sales. The goomba does not buy other people's things. If the goomba wanted your stuff, believe me, he'd have it already. He ain't paying good money for trash you're about to throw out.

There's lot of things the goomba dad isn't doing.
You can't be a goomba if:
You ever "get jiggy wid it."
You ever ate Chef Boy R Dee.
You ever ran out of olive oil or red wine.
You ever ate a frozen pizza.

You never grabbed your nuts to emphasize a point.

You never took anything to a pawn shop.

You never put your bookie's phone number on speed dial.

You might be a goomba if:

You've hot-wired a car.

You've taken lasagna to a movie theater.

You've taken a date to a car wash.

You've ever said, to a girl, "Pull my finger."

You've been at a dinner party where someone cracks their lobster claw with the butt of a gun.

There wasn't much socializing. The goomba wasn't taking everybody out for dinner in fancy restaurants. (My father took my mother to Manhattan for dinner once and he talked about it for the next twenty years. When they were dating, he'd take her to the Copacabana, or the Latin Quarter. Once they were married, they never went out again.) But this didn't mean no social life. The goomba family was very busy in those days with its social life. There were always these goomba events to attend. There was always a communion, or a baptism, or a wedding, or an engagement party, or a funeral. You'd go to at least one event every weekend where you'd see all your aunts and uncles and cousins and grandparents. All the events were very family oriented. And on Sunday, you'd have dinner with the family. Sometimes other nights, too. My friend Frank, when he was growing up, Sunday was the big dinner at his house. But on Friday, they'd go to his mother's father's house. And on Saturday, they'd go to his father's father's house. It was all family.

The big day was Father's Day. This was the special day for the goomba. He's going to be surrounded by his kids. Nobody's leaving the house on Father's Day. Other family members might come to

A happy goomba family. Wait 'til they start yelling at each other.

visit—his parents, his brothers, his sisters, their families. He's going to get a few gifts. Nothing fancy. Something practical. A razor. A new electric shaver. A tool of some kind. Socks.

For dinner it's his favorite meal. Whatever he wants. The sky is the limit. Usually, he got whatever he always had for Sunday dinner—because that was his favorite meal anyway.

During the summer the goomba dad always took the family on a big vacation. They'd go to the Catskills, or to Lake George, or out to Jersey to stay with Aunt Mary and Uncle Louie.

In the Catskills, they'd stay in the resorts. Most of the famous ones were the Jewish ones—the Concord, or Grossingers. The goombas didn't want to stay there—not because they didn't like the Jews, but because they didn't like the food. The goomba can't survive a week at Grossingers eating kishkas and gefilte fish.

The goomba wanted to stay at Villa Roma and eat big all week. The families that couldn't afford a week in the mountains sometimes went to Coney Island. There were these beach clubs there, Raven Hall and Washington Baths. You could buy a family membership for the summer, and feel like you were somebody special. You'd go for the day—there were no accommodations there for overnight—and have your own private place on the beach. You'd swim in the pool, eat in the restaurant, and go home late, after the city had gotten cool.

Some guys, they learned about sex from their dads. My father was too busy screwing up to tell me anything about anything. But my friend Mike, for example, his dad sat him down and laid it out.

When he was 15, his dad brought him into the bedroom and sat him down. He said, "How are you doing with the girls?" Mike said he was doing okay. His dad said, "Did you get laid yet?" Mike was so embarrassed he just looked at the floor. His dad said, "Did you get a blow job yet?" Mike was so embarrassed he couldn't even look at the floor. His dad said, "The first time that happens, your head is going to hit the ceiling."

Mike didn't know that was just an expression, so he was scared. He thought his head was literally going to hit the ceiling. Was that good? He wasn't sure. In fact, he had already had sex with a girl, but he couldn't tell his dad that. He thought the whole thing was embarrassing.

Later, he told his friends from the block what had happened. They said, "Your dad is the greatest!" They thought it was pretty cool that his dad could ask him about a blow job.

Mike's brother Frank told me his dad was always asking them questions about what they were doing, who they were seeing, all that. When Frank was 15, his father took him and his brother out to a nightclub. The boys both had fake IDs. Their father said, "I want to see you boys in action." He got them drinks and watched them try to pick up girls.

When Frank was starting to date girls, they'd call the house. And Frank's mother would think she recognized their voices. She'd say, "Angela, is that you?" And sometimes it would be some other girl. So Frank's dad would yell at his mother, "Don't say the name! Say 'honey,' or 'sweetie.' Don't say the name!" He didn't want his son's sex life to get screwed up. He was looking out for his boy.

One time I remember my friend's father got into a beef with this other kid's mother. The mother said something insulting about the kid. His father said, "You shut up!" Then her husband came outside. He said, "You can't talk that way in front of my woman!" My friend's father said, "You call *that* a woman?"

The two men started pushing each other. My friend tried to get in and separate them. He got knocked down. His dad went nuts. He clobbered the guy.

I didn't get any of that kind of instruction. Not about sex. Not about girls. Not about anything. Bottom line, I had to figure out how to be a dad on my own.

I got two beautiful daughters. So, I've learned a lot about being a dad. I've learned how to put them to bed at night, how to give them a bath, what they like to eat, what they like to wear, how to throw them birthday parties, how to get them ready for school, how to help them with their homework—the whole thing.

And the one thing I know best about being a dad is . . . it's scary! I'm scared all the time. Nothing scares me more than the safety of my kids. I can hardly think about it. I can't talk about it. When I think about my daughters, nothing scares me more than the idea of them getting hurt—physically hurt or emotionally hurt. If my daughter comes home and tells me someone hurt her feelings . . . it just kills me. I weigh 275 pounds, I'm pretty tough, and I just *melt*.

There was a kid who hit my daughter once or twice at school. My wife told me about it. It was the teacher's own son. My daughter was upset about it. I was upset about it. My wife had gone to the teacher and told her what had happened. The teacher said she would take care of it. Then her kid hit my daughter again.

I said to my wife, "I want you to go back and see the teacher again. Tell her this: 'If my daughter comes home again and tells me that your son hit her again, my husband is going to go to your house and take your husband and drag him into the yard and beat his ass in front of his kid.' Make sure she understands I am dead serious about this."

My wife went to see the teacher. She told her what I said to tell her. Guess what? No more hitting.

That's just the physical stuff. I worry more than that about the emotional stuff. I can't bear the idea that someone is going to hurt my daughter's feelings. That's because I remember being a kid and how certain things tore me up.

For example, the sports thing. I was on these Little League teams, like I said. Every weekend, you'd have to take a bus to get to the baseball game. Some kids, their fathers had cars. Other kids would take a bus. But the special kids, the kids who were the stars of the team and the coach's favorites, the coach would pick them up in his car and drive them to the game.

I was a good athlete, so I was usually one of those kids. But sometimes I'd screw up in the game. I'd make the error that cost us the game. I'd drop a ball. I'd strike out. Whatever. And then, suddenly, I wouldn't be in the coach's car going home. Suddenly there was no more room. I was on the bus, riding home alone. That was very hard on the young goomba.

When I was in high school, I tried out for the varsity basketball team. It was down to me and one guy for the last remaining spot. And they picked the other guy. This was the hardest thing that ever happened to me. I cried my eyes out. I thought my life was over.

I think of that now, and my daughters going through stuff like that, and I can't stand it. Many a time, I've said to my wife, "That's it! We're boarding up the house. No one's leaving until both girls are 40. We've got everything we need right here. No one's leaving!"

It's not just me. Every goomba takes his parenting duties very seriously. One way you can tell this is from the birthday parties.

I went to my first real goomba birthday party before I had kids myself. It was in New Jersey. I show up ready for a one-year-old's birthday party. I'm wearing jeans and a T-shirt. I've got a little present from Toys R Us. I'm expecting to see Barney and Elmo.

Instead, this thing is like a wedding. Everybody is wearing three-piece suits and nice dresses. There's fifty adults and about three kids. There's no pizza and hot dogs, either. It's Chateaubriand and champagne for everyone. There's no Barney and no Elmo. Instead, you got Rocco and Aunt Angelina with the big mole on her chin, and the same dance band that played at your wedding.

Not long after that, I get invited to a two-year-old's party in Las Vegas. I figure this will be different. It's Vegas. It's not gonna be like Bensonhurst. I think it's going to be a backyard barbecue kind of thing. But the address turns out to be a catering hall. It's 11:00 on a Saturday morning. Everyone is in three-piece suits and nice dresses—again! There's hardly any kids there, either. It's all grown-ups. There's a fancy meal and music. This party had to cost thousands of dollars. I've been to weddings that weren't this fancy.

Now I get it. There's the baptism, then the first couple of birthdays, then the first communion party, then the confirmation party, then the sweet sixteen party, then the wedding . . . It's all huge. (And the guest list never changes, by the way. You see the same group at every party for twenty-five years running.) The goomba has to have a big party. He has to show off, too. He wants to keep up with the Joneses. Or the Russos. Or whatever.

Being a good father is very important to the goomba. Not that they're always good at it:

♥ When a goomba's son asks him how little boys and girls are "made," the goomba says, "They gotta whack somebody."

♥ When a goomba's kid opens a lemonade stand on the block, the goomba says, "Nice stand, but you better get some insurance."

♥ When it's Father-Son Day at school, the goomba makes sure he and his kid are wearing matching sweat suits.

♥ When it's "Take Your Child to Work Day," the goomba makes sure his son has a good day at the track, and gets some nice attention from the blonde with the big hooters at Gino's G Spot.

♥ When his kid's pet turtle dies, the goomba buries the thing in the backyard and pours lye over it.

Those may not be the best ways to do it. But it's the goomba way.

Every goomba is supposed to hope that one day he will be the father of a strapping young goomba boy. As soon as he gets married, the talking starts: "What about kids?" As soon as the wife is pregnant, the talking starts: "You're going to have a beautiful baby boy!" Remember the scene in *The Godfather?* The clumsy, stuttering goomba soldier, on the wedding day of Don Corleone's daughter, says, "I hope your daughter will soon have a child, and that it will be a healthy masculine child." This is supposed to be the central relationship in a goomba's life—the relationship with the son who will inherit everything from him.

Myself, I got two daughters. In some ways, raising them is easier than raising boys. You don't spend as much time getting stitches in the emergency room, for one thing. And when they get older, they're probably not going to wind up robbing liquor stores, getting other girls pregnant, or calling from Miami to say they're in jail.

But raising daughters is still difficult. They're girls, first of all, which means they're like your mother and your wife. You have to be delicate because they're sensitive. And they know that if they start crying they can pretty much get anything they want out of you. So you have to be fair, and firm, and know when to say "no." Here are some examples of firm, fair parenting.

Things a goomba will never say to his daughter:
"Of course you can get a tattoo."
"I think guys on Harleys are sexy, too."
"Quit school and go to work as a stripper? Why not?"
"Elope? Sure. Your mother won't mind."

I'm lucky to have daughters. One thing I don't have to struggle with is the whole macho kid thing. I know some goomba dads who are very proud of how tough their kids are. They say things like, "I was a rough and tumble guy, and I turned out all right. I want my kid to be tough, too." So they get their kids in karate and make sure they know how to kick and punch and attack.

Things a goomba will never say to his son:
"Of course I'll buy you a Barbie doll."
"I wore dresses myself as a boy."
"Baseball? That's for sissies."
"Why should you work? I'll support you forever."

I don't think it's a good idea to raise kids to become tough guys. It can backfire. My brother got into a fight with a kid when he was little. My brother hit him with his fist. The kid came back and hit my brother with a wrench. My mother went to yell at the other kid's parents. The father said, "I taught my kid, if someone hits you, you hit him back with something worse."

Like that scene with Sean Connery in Brian De Palma's *The Untouchables*. Connery tells his men, "If he's got a knife, you get a gun. If he sends one of your men to the hospital, you send one of his men to the morgue . . ." That's great advice, except when your kid winds up in the hospital, or the morgue.

I think all the emphasis on sports is a little insane, too. Of course it's great for kids to get exercise, and play games, and do all that. It's fun for them. My kids have been on all kinds of teams, and I hope they continue. But I think making a big deal out of it is a bad idea. Some kids are going to grow up to be Serena Williams or Tiger Woods. But most kids are not. When I was in high school, I was around a lot of guys who thought being on the team was *everything*. It was the most important thing that ever was. They'd ignore their studies, or their friends, or their families, to make sure they stayed on the team.

I'm telling you, from experience, there's many a high school jock sitting in a bar someplace, right now, crying in his beer. He was captain of the football team. He was a star! But now he's working a minimum-wage job and he can't make ends meet, and he can't figure out what went wrong.

Some of the goomba dads like to make their kids perform, too. I hate that. I can see the kids squirming every time the dad says, "Come on, show Uncle Steve how you sing. Show Uncle Steve how you dance." Or they think it's funny to make their little tiny kids say dirty words.

I think that's all pathetic. I know these goomba dads are all very proud, but they treat their kids like performing chimps. You go over to the house, and suddenly they're auditioning for *Star Search*.

The true goomba will do anything to keep his family together. From the time he's little, he knows one day he's going to grow up and get married and have little goomba kids. All around him that's what he sees. Huge families. Sunday dinner with thirty people at the table. All his cousins. All his friends' cousins. It's all *famiglia*.

Every once in a while it doesn't work out, but not very often. I don't have any statistics to back this up, but I think the goomba divorce rate is way below the national average. It's higher in Las Vegas—where if your husband looks at you funny across the breakfast table, you file for divorce before lunchtime. I think it's higher because there is no social pressure. Back in the neighborhood, where everyone on the block knows you and your mother and your father and your wife and her mother and father, where 200 people within a four-square-block radius were all at your wedding, and half of those people were at your parent's wedding, and half of *those* people were at your *grandparents'* wedding, you're going to be a little hesitant to bring in the lawyers. You're going to try a little harder to make it work. You're going to give it a little more time. You're going to stay together, maybe, until you forget what it was you wanted to get a divorce over.

The goomba family tries very hard, in other words, to stay together. Sometimes they try too hard. The father drinks too much, but they try. The father gambles too much, but they try. The father's a womanizer with a *goomar*, but they try.

We had troubles in my family, too. My father wasn't around all that much. He was a drinker and a gambler, and he wasn't always a good provider. But still my mother stuck by him. Even years later, after he had died, she would

Forget the clothes; you gotta love the wallpaper.

get sentimental when something nice happened and say, "If only your father were here to see this! He'd be so proud!"

No, he wouldn't. This guy didn't even come to my college graduation. He said he was tired. I was the first man in my family—ever!—to graduate from college. Can you imagine missing that? With my kids, I try not to miss anything.

Not that I enjoy it all the time. I take my kids to the movies, and sometimes the movies they want to see are not exactly *The Godfather*. I go and buy the candy and the popcorn and the soda and we sit there and watch Michael Keaton play *Frosty the Snowman*. At the end, when Frosty melted, my two-year-old daughter was crying so hard I almost died. And the comedies are no better. We went to see *Spice World* with the Spice Girls. Is there anything worse than that?

Actually, there is. I did it recently. I would sit through six complete episodes of *Hey Arnold* rather than sit again through Roberto Benigni's *Pinnochio*. There is nothing in the world more unpleasant than that. And I did it once already.

The goomba suffers for his family.

But what a payoff.

For example, my wife just turned 40. I was out of town on her birthday. To celebrate, she went out with my two daughters and one of her best friends, to a Mexican restaurant we go to a lot. They had a big Mexican meal. When the check came, my oldest daughter grabbed it and said, "Happy birthday, Mom. We're buying dinner."

The two girls, who are 11 and 7 years old, had decided to pool their allowance money and buy a birthday dinner for their mother. The check came to something like $50. My wife's friend said, "I can't let two little girls buy me dinner." My wife said, "You have to." She was all choked up. Her daughters insisted on picking up the check.

They're Daddy's little girls. Little goombas! Two chips off the old block.

A Fool for Love:
The Two-Timing
Goomba

Even when a goomba is cheating, there's rules. There's cheating etiquette.

*L*ike I said before, the goomba is full of love—sometimes too much love for just one woman. Sometimes the goomba is going to have a girlfriend, even if he's already married. Sometimes he has a steady girlfriend, but he cheats on *her*. Sometimes, to be honest, a married man will cheat on his wife with his *goomar,* and he'll cheat on his *goomar* with another girl. Maybe there's some guy somewhere who's even cheating on the girl he's cheating on his *goomar* with. That's just plain greedy. Nobody really needs more than two. More than two is unnecessary.

I don't fool around myself, but I know a lot of guys who do. Or who would like to. Some goombas think you gotta have a *goomar*—the little something on the side. Some goombas think you're not a real man unless you've got a wife and a family and a hot little number tucked away in an apartment somewhere.

Not every goomba has one. Not every goomba needs one. And some guys, it's amazing they could even get *one* girl to sleep with them.

Whatever the case, this is an important part of goomba love. With some goombas, it's the whole story on goomba love. With some of these guys, it's an obsession.

I know a guy who got laid on his honeymoon—and I don't mean with his wife. He got married, and he and the new bride went to the

Bahamas. On the third day, his wife went for a massage and manicure at the hotel spa. The goomba went down to the pool to work
on his tan. He gets talking to this girl by the pool, and the next
thing you know he's up in her room. He's been married three days,
and he's already cheating on his new wife.

I know another guy, speaking of the Bahamas, who's been cheating on his wife for twenty years. When he takes his family to the
Bahamas, he always stays in the same hotel. And he always gets a
room for the *goomar.* He puts his wife and kids in a big suite on the
twentieth floor. He parks the girlfriend in a room on the tenth
floor. Every day he tells the wife, "I'm going for a walk," and goes to
visit the *goomar.*

That's nuts, right? And it's kind of sick. But it also makes a bit of
sense. The goomba is cheating on his wife, but he's doing it with a
little class and a little style, and he's taking care that no one gets hurt.

Even when the goomba is cheating, there's rules. There's cheating etiquette. Certain things are acceptable. Certain things are not.

The goomba will never bring his girlfriend into his wife's bed.
He never brings the girl home. He never brings the *goomar* over to
the house. That would be disrespecting his wife and his family.

Instead, the goomba is going to go to a hotel. And not just any
hotel. If he's from New York, he's going to Jersey. If he's from Jersey,
he's going to New York.

The goomba will never take his girlfriend to a place where he goes
with his wife and family, either. That's disrespectful, too. If he fre-
quents a certain restaurant with the wife and kids, he won't go there
with the *goomar.* The waiters and the bartenders would really look
down on a guy who did that. He's disrespecting his wife, in public.

A goomba will never talk his wife down in public, either. Even if
he's out with the *goomar* and her friends. He'll never speak against
his wife in public. Again, it's disrespectful.

A goomba will never hit on another goomba's girlfriend. That's another unspoken rule. Another man's *goomar* is strictly off limits (You remember what happened to the councilman on *The Sopranos* when he fell in love with Tony's former *goomar*—and they'd been history for months.) And, among the *goomars*, there is an unspoken rule that you never go for another girl's boyfriend.

The relationship with the goomba and the *goomar* could probably fill a whole book. In some ways, it's just like the relationship between the goomba and his wife. There are certain things, for example, that the goomba will never tell either of them.

Things a goomba will never tell his *goomar:*
♥ What he does.
♥ What he earns.
♥ Where he lives.
♥ How he feels.

A goomba isn't going to get all touchy-feely emotional about anything. A goomba with a girlfriend on the side is still a goomba.

Things a goomba will never say to his *goomar:*
"I need a hug."
"How come you never call me at the house?"
"Do you think I look fat in these pantyhose?"
"Of course I'm still having sex with my wife."
"You want breast implants? What the hell for?"

There are levels of cheating, too, and that can be confusing. For example, my friend Frank can't be with another girl if he's wearing underwear that his steady girlfriend gave him.

He's serious about this. One time he found himself in a certain situation with a girl he had just met. They were in a car. It was hot and heavy. She was pulling his pants off. He suddenly realized he was wearing the special underwear his girlfriend had given him for Christmas. And he couldn't continue. He made the girl stop.

At first, this seems ridiculous. He's already being unfaithful, right? I asked him what the difference was.

He said, "This girl is nothing to me. It's just sex. I'm not going to go out with her again. I'm not going to take her on vacation to Hawaii. I'm not even going to take her to dinner. So, what I'm doing poses no threat to my relationship. I love my girlfriend. That's not going to change. This is just a little sex."

So what's the problem with the underwear?

"Being with the girl doesn't disrespect my girlfriend," Frank says. "But I'm wearing the special underwear. This would disrespect the *gift.*"

It's like honor among thieves, which may or may not exist. Among the goombas and the *goomars,* though, it's real. It has to be. The goomba is taking a real chance, having a girlfriend. And the *goomar* has a lot at stake, too. The goomba may be her meal ticket. He may be paying her rent. She may be in love with the guy. So nobody wants to rock the boat.

Including the goomba wife. This is maybe hard to understand, but in a lot of goomba marriages, the wife probably knows that the goomba has a girlfriend on the side. And in a lot of goomba marriages, the wife accepts that. She doesn't want to know about it. She doesn't want to hear about it. But she accepts it.

Why? It's a tradition. Their fathers cheated on their mothers. Their grandfathers cheated on their grandmothers. Maybe the wife is just a housewife, and she doesn't know anything else. She's got a couple of kids, and no money of her own. What's she going to do? She's got no place else to go. As long as he's not rubbing her face in it, she might accept it.

Also, some of these wives don't like sex, or they don't like as much sex as their husbands do, or they don't want the kind of sex their husbands want. Some of them, you see what happens after they get married, it's like they're raising a flag that says "No Sex!" on it. They stop being romantic when they get that ring. For some women, it's a relief to stop having sex. And they know the girlfriend on the side keeps the goomba happy.

As long as he's behaving himself, everybody enjoys the benefits. The goomba might buy a gift for the *goomar*. But then he feels guilty, so he buys the same gift for his wife. And vice versa. I know one guy who, when he buys a piece of jewelry, he always buys *two*—identical necklaces, or bracelets, or watches, or whatever. One is for the wife, one is for the girlfriend. Everybody wins. If the goomba is having a good time with the *goomar*, he's a happy guy at home.

When I was a young man, cheating was so common that we all joked about it. My friend Charles tells this story about a guy who's in bed with this married woman. The phone rings. She answers it and says, "Hello? Okay. Fine." Then she hangs up. The guy says, "Who was that?" The woman says, "My husband. He called to say he was going to be out late—with you."

If the goomba is doing okay, he's going to take care of everybody. He's going to pay the *goomar*'s rent. He'll take care of her family, and he'll buy her gifts. Maybe he'll buy her a dress. He'll take her shopping. He'll say, "You want to go out Saturday? Here's $500. Go buy yourself a nice outfit."

And he's going to be taking care of his own family and buying gifts for his wife, too. The goomba is a big-hearted, generous guy. He's gonna do the right thing.

The trouble is, sometimes the *goomar* wants to return the favor. She's generous too. Her man buys her a bracelet, she wants to buy something for him. Jewelry is always nice, so she'll buy the goomba a pinkie ring, or maybe a watch.

The goomba is very touched. This is very sweet. But, what's he going to tell his wife? If she sees the new ring, or the new watch, he's got to have an explanation. So most guys have a story. Guys will say things, like

"I won it in a poker game."

"This guy owed me money. He gave me this instead."

"I was at the track and my exacta came in. I went a little nuts."

"I was in Atlantic City, and I hit the jackpot. I decided to buy myself something to celebrate."

The goomba is always dancing, here, trying to find some excuse. The smart goomba, if he's going to make up that kind of story, he buys one more piece of jewelry to go along with his new watch. He tells his wife the lie about the watch, and then he says, "And I picked up something for you, too." No wife is going to complain too much if she gets a nice bracelet out of it.

The goomba's worst nightmare is getting caught cheating. Every goomba can tell you a horror story about this—about him, or his friend, and the big showdown with the wife. Or the *goomar*. (Heaven help the goomba who gets caught!)

There are lots of methods for staying out of trouble. The first one is to know when you're *in* trouble. Here are some things to watch out for.

How to know if your wife thinks you're cheating:

She's paying attention when you make love.

You come home to find her sniffing your underpants.

There's a private investigator snooping around—and he's not the one you hired to follow *her*.

If you think your wife is suspicious, watch out what you say. The wrong word can give you away faster than anything else. For instance, the savvy goomba won't say things like "That's the second nicest ass I've seen this week," or "Honey, how do you get lipstick off of silk undershorts?"

If you're sure your wife is suspicious, be very careful what you do. The average goomba wife is very jealous. If you give her the evidence she's looking for, she'll come at you with everything she's got—and she might wind up with everything *you've* got.

What *not* to do if your wife thinks you're cheating:

Come home wearing different clothes than you left in.

Come home wearing jewelry your wife didn't buy you.

Take your *goomar* to your parents' house for dinner.

Some guys have very elaborate schemes for not getting caught. I have one friend, for example. He's a married guy. But he's quite a ladies man, too. So he's always meeting this girl or that girl, and having these little flings. He doesn't want his wife to find out, of course. So he's got a system for keeping everything straight.

When he meets a girl, and makes a date, he does it in code. If he meets a waitress named Mary and makes a date to meet at the Hard Rock Hotel, he writes in his little book, "Marty, hiring waitresses at Hard Rock." If her number is 367-0254, he writes in his book, "367-4520."

A girl named Lynn becomes a guy named Lenny. Angela is Angelo. JoAnn becomes Joey. That way, he keeps it all straight, and no one is any the wiser. If his wife should find his book, it'll look like he just makes notes about doing favors for guys or just going about his business. "Joey, Caesar's, call Tuesday about massage." No one but him knows that means he's going to book a room at Caesar's on Tuesday to have sex with a massage therapist named JoAnn.

And if she gets suspicious, and calls the number to check, she won't get Lenny or Angelo or Joey. She'll get some broad. And then my friend will say, "What do you know? I must have wrote the number down wrong."

Another guy I know has a special slang that he uses with his *goomar*. He'll call her on the phone and say, "Yo, Bobby. I'm thinking about getting a haircut. Can you fit me in tomorrow about ten?" He might make this call in front of his wife, sitting in the living room, watching TV. He's making a date with his girlfriend. Can you fit me in! You bet she can!

Or he'll call and say he needs an oil change. He needs his tires rotated. He needs his pants pressed. He does all of this right in front of his wife. He's a real comedian, that guy. But as far as I know, he's never been caught.

Since the invention of the cell phone, this kind of thing isn't as necessary as it used to be. It's a huge advancement in goomba cheating. Many a goomba owes his entire love life to the cell phone. Before that, he was always going down to the corner for a pack of cigarettes just so he could get to a public telephone. For the goomba who didn't smoke, this was even more difficult. He was sneaking around just in order to make a date to sneak around. Now, it's very convenient. He can dial the *goomar* from the comfort of his own home, and make a date, and sound like he's just making an appointment to get his hair cut.

One guy I know has a special cell phone that only his *goomar* can use. It looks just like his regular cell phone, but it has a different ringer. And the girlfriend is the only one who has the number. When it rings, he knows it's the girlfriend calling. If he's at home, he'll let it ring.

Another guy I know has three cell phones. One is for his wife and his business. He gives that number to everybody. Another one is for his *goomar* and a couple of close friends. No one else has that number. The third phone is for new girls that he has just met. No one else gets that number—not the wife, not the *goomar*, not the best friend. Each of the phones is a different color, and each of the phones has a different ring, of course. When that third phone goes off, *hurray!* That's good news coming in. The only trick is remember which ring is which.

One smart guy I know tells any girl he's going to go out with—any girl that isn't his steady girlfriend, I mean—not to wear any perfume. He lays it straight out. He tells them he lives with a girl who's really jealous, and if she smells perfume on him he'll get in trouble. If the girl shows up on the date smelling like perfume, he won't take her out.

Another guy I know keeps detailed notes, but also in code, of where he's been and who with. That way, he doesn't trip over himself taking the same girl to the same place twice, or taking his wife someplace he's just been with some girl. If you get sloppy about that stuff, it can bite you in the ass.

Once when I was working as a bouncer in this club I got to know this sort of high roller. He came in one Saturday night with a girl, and they had a big time. Spent a lot of money. Bought drinks for everybody. I wasn't paying too much attention to who he was with. But I remembered him, when he came back, again with a girl, a few nights later. I said to him, "You had a nice time Saturday night?" He mumbled something and walked away from me. A little while later he came over, alone, and said, "What the fuck are you trying to do to me?" He was with his wife when he came in on Saturday, it turns out, and now he's back with his *goomar.*

Most guys are careful the same way about what hotels they go to with their girlfriends, and what hotels they go to with the girls they cheat on the girlfriends with. The important thing is you don't want to be seen, so you don't go where people you know are going to see you.

When I was young, the big cheating places were the Golden Gate Inn and the Jade East. These were places with short stays. You could rent a room for three or four hours. The Golden Gate is in Sheepshead Bay. The Jade East is in Queens. These were the famous goomba cheating places.

But those places might be too close if you live in Queens or Sheepshead Bay. So you go to Manhattan. You stay in the big places, if you've got the bread. You stay at the Hilton, or the Sheraton, if you've got a couple of hundred bucks to throw down for the night.

Otherwise, you might save a few bucks and go out on Route One, where there's millions of motels. You might go out near the Meadowlands, or near Newark Airport.

Or, to save time and not get seen, maybe you go to Staten Island. For a guy from Brooklyn, that's right in the middle, halfway between the city and Jersey. And not as expensive as Manhattan.

Remember, the money thing is important. We're not talking Wall Street guys here. We're not talking Donald Trump. We're talking blue collar guys, for the most part. The goomba is making 75G a year, max, so he can't afford $200 a night hotel rooms, two times a week. He can't afford the little hideaway love nest on the Upper East Side. Some WASP guys might have one of those. Some Wall Street guys maybe. Not the goomba.

At the most, he may have a little apartment, if he's got a steady *goomar*. But again he does this in a place where he's not going to get seen. He doesn't get a place in Little Italy. He doesn't get something right in the neighborhood where he eats, where his friends go. He gets something up Columbus Avenue, where there aren't too many goombas. He doesn't want people knowing his business.

Some guys play it pretty loose.

I've got one buddy who has been with the same woman for twenty-five years—in addition to his wife, who he's been married to for almost the same amount of time. This guy loves his wife. He loves his family. But he also loves this other woman. So he takes care of all of them. He makes sure everybody gets their fair share. And he's got it down to a science. You could set your watch by this guy, by the schedule he's on with the wife and the other woman.

Every Monday he tells his wife he's going to Westchester on business. He goes to Westchester and meets the girlfriend. They spend the day together. Then he tells the girlfriend he's got business back in the city. He goes home. The next day, he tells his wife he'll be at the office. At lunch, he goes out to meet the girlfriend. At the end of the day, he takes his wife and kids out for dinner. The next day, he tells the people in his office that he's got to see some suppliers. He goes back with the girlfriend. On Thursday, he actually goes to work, and stays there all day. He has to! So far, he hasn't done anything all week but fool around. He spends Friday night at home with the wife, and maybe some friends come over for dinner. Come Saturday, he's so beat that he tells his wife he's going down to Florida for a few days, to get some sun and take it easy.

The girlfriend is already down there. He spends the weekend with her.

Every year, for twenty years, he tells his wife that him and Charlie and Rocco are going skiing in Colorado. This guy's never been on skis in his life. Instead, he and his two buddies and their three girlfriends take a few suites in Las Vegas. They spend four days hanging around, drinking and gambling, and getting a suntan by the pool. Then he goes home to his family.

There was a time when this guy had other girls, too. He was cheating on the wife and the girlfriend both. Now, he says he doesn't have the energy to keep up with the wife and the girlfriend, and keep chasing the outside broads too. So he takes it easy.

I have heard horror stories about guys getting caught. Some of them are funny. Some of them are tragic. All of them involve a guy who got a little greedy, or a little lazy, and got nabbed. Or just got unlucky.

My friend Charlie worked at the Hilton. There was a captain there who was fooling around behind his wife's back, with a cocktail waitress who worked in the pits—where the craps and blackjack tables are. Everyone knew what was going on, including the wife. One night she came in to the casino and stormed over to the pits, carrying this big sack over her shoulder. She went straight up to the cocktail waitress and dumped the bag on the floor and said, "There! Do his laundry, too!"

He and the wife broke up shortly after that. The captain married the cocktail waitress. Unfortunately, my friend Charlie says, he was a player. He fooled around on the cocktail waitress, and she left him too. Forever after, he was single. And happy.

Another guy who was a friend of mine, his wife figured out he was cheating. She figured out where he was going to be one night. He was having dinner in a restaurant with his girlfriend. The wife came in and started screaming, really berating him, in public. "You pig! You lying bastard! You have a tiny cock! You're a lousy lay! And to think I've been washing your shit-stained underwear for fifteen years!"

Needless to say the marriage was over. And so was this guy's reputation. Now everybody in town knows he's got a small dick, is lousy in bed, and leaves streaks in his underpants. What a humiliation!

Another friend of mine works in a club. He was in the balcony late one night, after the last show, getting a blow job from some girl he had just met. His girlfriend came in and walked straight up to the balcony. She took one look at what was going on and started screaming. She threw her drink on the girl's head.

My friend didn't bat an eye. He said, "Are you finished? Then get the hell out of here."

GOOMBA PERSONAL AD

NICKNAME: Vinny the Mink.

OCCUPATION: Juice man.

LAST GREAT BOOK I READ: *I'm Okay, You're a Douchebag.*

#1 THING YOU SHOULD KNOW ABOUT ME: I tip big after sex.

THINGS I CAN'T LIVE WITHOUT: Sinatra. My tailor. My
mother's meatballs.

MY FAVORITE ROMANTIC SONG: The thing from that Ragu
commercial.

MY IDEAL MATE IS: Female. Breathing. Under 200 pounds.

Sometimes the tables get turned on the poor goomba who fools
around.

I know a guy, an older guy, who'd been married a long time. He's
got a thing for hookers. He's got hookers in every city you can
name. When he leaves town on business, he goes to town with the
hookers. And this is going on forever. Like, for twenty-five years,
he's cheating on his wife with the hookers.

And he's not even discreet about it. All his friends know. He
talks about it all the time. He complains about his wife all the time,
too. He says, "I got to go home to that fat bitch now. My fat fucking wife is waiting for me at home."

Goombas don't like that. They don't like to hear a man talking
down his wife that way. But that's how this guy talked.

So one day, the goomba has plans to go on this business trip.
He's all excited. There's this new girl he's going to see. He's made it
an extra long trip, so he can spend time with her. And his wife is
going to take advantage of this long trip. She's decided to get some
plastic surgery. She's having all this stuff done—her face, her boobs,
everything. It's going to be $11,000 worth.

The goomba is happy. He can go away for three weeks and know that his wife is going to be busy recuperating from the surgery.

So he goes. He has a great time. But he gets a little bored. The girl is not that interesting. He doesn't meet any new girls. So he comes home a few days early.

The wife isn't there. He waits. She doesn't come home. He waits. She doesn't come home that night. He waits. He's going crazy, but he waits. She finally comes in the next morning. The goomba is half nuts. He demands an explanation.

The wife confesses. She's got a boyfriend. She's had a boyfriend, for a long time. She's even supporting the guy, with her husband's money. She's paying the guy's rent.

The goomba is horrified. He says, "How could you do this to me?"

The wife laughs. She says, "You? With all your *whoo-ah* girl-friends? Why shouldn't I have a little fun too?"

That's the end. The goomba is crushed.

Another guy I know—he had it even worse.

He was living with this girl. He really loved her. One time he was out of town on business. His business ended early. He was excited because he could come home early and surprise his girlfriend. It was a Saturday night, and that was her night off. So he called from the airport. No answer. He called her cell phone. No answer.

When he gets back to Las Vegas, he calls from the airport. A man answers. He says, "Can I speak to Cynthia?" The man says, "What?" My friend says, "Never mind, I got the wrong number." The man says, "No. Cynthia's here. She's asleep. Hang on a minute."

My friend hurries home. He lets himself into the apartment. He goes into his bedroom. There's his girlfriend, naked, passed out on the bed, sleeping next to this guy in his underwear. The guy wakes up. He sees my friend. He gets out of bed. My friend is actually standing on the guy's clothes, lying on the floor. The guy looks at my friend, looks at his clothes, and goes into the other room. My friend hears him call someone on the phone. He says, "I'm at Cynthia's. Come pick me up."

My friend is dying. He doesn't know what to do. But he gets a plan. This girl Cynthia made him get an AIDS test before she would sleep with him. She was very paranoid about using a condom. So he looks around to see if there's a condom lying around. There isn't. So he opens one, from the bathroom drawer. He stretches it out so it looks used, and he sort of drapes it over the waste paper basket in the bathroom. The next morning, when his girlfriend goes to the bathroom, she's going to see it. She's going to know he saw it, too.

The next day, she swears nothing happened. My friend wants to believe it. But he can't. So he has her telephone forwarded to his telephone. He makes a copy of her outgoing answering machine message, and records it as his own outgoing answering machine message. Pretty soon he starts getting calls, from the guy.

"What are we going to do about last night? We gotta get our story straight."

"Please call me back. Don't let this break up our relationship."

"Why aren't you calling? After all we've been through this last year, please don't leave me now."

The guy doesn't want to believe what he's hearing. So he plays the messages for his girlfriend. She still denies everything. She says the guy just drove her home because she was drunk. He's got a crush on her. He's fantasizing about this relationship he thinks they have. It's all a lie.

So my friend plays the trump card. He says, "I found a rubber, in the bathroom, and it was used."

The girl says, "If that's true, then he raped me!"

My friend is so relieved. She didn't sleep with him!

But the guy keeps calling. So, my friend sits the girl down and makes her call the guy back. He's listening to everything she says.

He's making her ask questions. He's got the questions written down. He's making her ask the questions, and listening to the answers. And there's one question she won't ask. My friend is jabbing his finger at the paper where he's written the questions. Finally, she says, "If we didn't have sex, why did you leave a used condom in the bathroom?"

And the guy says, "A condom? We've been sleeping together for six months. When did I ever use a condom?"

The end. Over. Out. Done. My friend was heartbroken. He didn't go out with anyone for, like, a week.

WARNING SIGNS

It can be hard to take when the person you're cheating with cheats on you, so here are some warning signs. Pay attention, and you won't get burned like my friend did.

How to tell if your *goomar* is cheating on you:

She's wearing jewelry that you didn't buy for her.

She suddenly has plans for Friday night, and they don't include you.

She tells you she has to work on the weekend—but she doesn't have a job.

She stops pretending to enjoy sex with you.

She starts acting like she actually has a life.

One problem for the goomba who's cheating is the incredible jealousy of the goomba woman. They are just as territorial as the goomba men. Maybe more territorial, since they are going to be jealous of just one man. The goomba is spreading the love all around. The goomba-ette, she's just got one guy to be jealous of. So the jealousy is intense.

When the goomba couple or the goomba family goes out, many a goomba will find his wife staring at everything *he's* staring at. The wife will say, "What are *you* looking at?" If you're looking at some other broad's ass, you're busted. The wife will say, "I see. You like a skinny girl with no ass and her eyes too close together." She'll say, "Is that what you want? A *puttana* with her tits hanging out for the whole world to see?"

A goomba couple for over fifty years and still in love.

Pity the poor goomba whose woman sees her man getting hit on when she's around. The goomba broad ain't gonna sit down for that. She's going to strike back. If some girl comes up and talks to her man, she's gonna get busy. Even if it's just a girl who's a friend. She won't wait to find out.

She'll say, "This is my husband. Take your thin fucking lips and your flat fucking ass and go back on the other side of the bar."

Usually, if the goomba is going to cheat on his wife with a steady *goomar,* he's going to pick someone who's the opposite of his wife. If the wife is very demure, he's looking for someone who's wild and crazy. If his wife is a screamer, he's looking for someone shy and quiet. He can't afford to have two screamers in his life. He doesn't want headaches on both ends.

Most of the time, the goomba will have a combative relationship with the wife, and a smooth relationship with the *goomar.* He'll fight with the wife, and run to the *goomar* for comfort. He'll raise the family with the wife, and go have fun with the *goomar.*

But not always. I know guys who have to go home to get away from their girlfriends. I know guys who have to go stay in a hotel, to get away from them both.

The worst of all is the goomba who's got a jealous *goomar.* Here's where the ethics of cheating get really weird. The goomba is allowed to cheat, but only with the *goomar.* This is the accepted rule. This kind of cheating is almost institutional. It's the social norm. The *goomar* isn't jealous of the wife because the wife came first. As long as the goomba is treating everyone right, everyone will be happy.

But if the goomba starts cheating on the *goomar* . . . this is the nightmare. The *goomar* can be much more jealous than the wife, even. She's got less ownership of the goomba, so she guards what she's got with her life. If she finds out there's another girlfriend involved, believe me, that ain't rolling off her chest. She's going to kick some ass. She's going to make some trouble.

First of all, she's going to tell everyone. All the *goomars* are friends. When the guy goes out with his girlfriend on the weekend, he and his friends all go out together. So the *goomars* all get to know each other really well. They socialize when the goombas aren't around. So, all the girls in the circle are going to know. All their boyfriends are going to know. Pretty soon, it's all over the neighborhood.

This can complicate the goomba's life. First of all, if the *goomar* gets really upset and drops him, he might have trouble finding a new girlfriend. Because *now* he's got a reputation as a guy who cheats. He's not dependable.

Worse, the *goomar* might even make some trouble with the wife. This is the worst thing that can ever happen to the goomba: His wife and his *goomar* team up against him, both of them betrayed, over some piece of tail he's got on the side. Then the goomba is in a world of pain.

Ultimately, the goomba has to trust the *goomar* as much as he trusts his wife. He's putting a lot at stake, fooling around. If that blows up, it could wreck his marriage. It could cut him off from his children. He's going to be careful about who he picks and what he does.

God forbid it should go wrong. You remember what happened in *The Sopranos* with Gloria Trillo? She and Tony had a thing. It stopped working. She didn't want it to end. She wanted revenge. She was threatening to bust up Tony's marriage with Carmela. So she got a visit from a very scary guy who explained to her that it was not in her best interests to continue with that line of approach.

He told her he was only going to warn her once. If she continued to cause trouble for Tony, he'd be back. He pointed to his own mug, and said, "This will be the last face you see on earth if you ever go near Tony Soprano and his family again."

TURNING THE TABLES: THE CHEATING GOOMBA-ETTE

The goomba girl is a very loyal girl. She will stand by her man, no matter what, forever. In most cases. Sometimes, though, something goes wrong. The goomba begins to suspect that something is not right in his world. He begins to suspect that someone is fooling around. Someone who isn't him. Now the tables have turned. The goomba begins to suspect that maybe his wife is the one doing the sneaking around.

Should he have seen it coming? Maybe. Usually, there are subtle hints that something is going on.

HOW TO TELL IF YOUR WIFE IS
CHEATING ON *YOU:*

She changes the initials on all your towels—to your best
   friend's.

She says she has to work late—but she doesn't have a job.

Her clothes smell like cigars—and you don't smoke.

The name she calls out when you're making love is your
   bookie's.

She's going shopping—with your *goomar.*

She's smiling again.

This is the lowest thing. For the goomba to imagine his wife seeing another man, this is the hardest thing in the world.

Even when the relationship is over, the goomba is going to try and do the right thing. I've heard stories about WASP guys breaking up in horrible ways. Like, they send the girl a letter. They leave the girl a telephone message. They send the girl a fax.

The goomba would never do that. It's not manly. It's dishonest. The goomba is going to lay it out there.

I have a friend who called me recently. He needed some help. He told me he was breaking up with the girl he was living with. He had met someone else, someone younger and more exciting. It wasn't that he didn't love his girlfriend anymore. It was just . . . over. But she was a great girl. She had been loyal to him. So he didn't want to just split.

He said, "I'm giving her 20 grand, so she can get an apartment and set herself up. But I want to get her a job someplace, too, so I know she'll be all right. I need you to help me get her a good job in one of the clubs."

That's a good goomba. He's ditching the broad, but he wants to make sure she's going to be taken care of.

And even after the breakup, the goomba has rules about the new girl. He won't take her to the places he went with the old girl. He won't introduce her around right away to his friends. That would be disrespectful. He can't let the old girlfriend know he was seeing this other girl when they were still together. He's got to do it slow. It might be a month before he goes out in public on a real date with the new girl. And if someone sees him, he might say, "Oh, that was a cousin of mine from back east." Or, "That was a girl from work." Otherwise, he's disrespecting the girl he was with.

Even for the guys who are not strictly cheating, the goomba etiquette comes into play. One of my best friends has a thing for showgirls and strippers. He takes them out, and he brings them home. But afterwards, he doesn't really want them around. He wants to go to sleep, alone. But he doesn't want to be rude.

So he'll say, "It's late. You should probably get home."

But usually the girls want to stay overnight. So my friend will take a hundred bucks and put it on the nightstand. He'll say, "You should go. Here's a couple bucks for a cab."

Nine times out of ten, the girl will glance over at the money and then, in about two minutes, say, "You know, it's late. I really should be going."

He could just throw them out. But he's a goomba with nice manners. He'd rather give them a hundred bucks to make them go away.

A Time for Love:
The Romantic
Goomba

Valentine's Day is a very big deal for the goomba. He's a sentimental guy.

*E*very day is a holiday in the life of a true goomba. Something special is always going on. The goomba don't like routine. If you look at his Day Planner—if he even *had* a Day Planner—it would say things like, "Wednesday, Drinks with Vito. Thursday, Lunch with Angelo. Friday, Dinner with Sal and Paulie."

The goomba is a very social guy. He even belongs to a Social Club. That's where he goes for his coffee. The average guy might meet a friend at the golf course or Home Depot, but not the goomba. He's meeting people at the Italian-American Social League, or the local diner, or the neighborhood candy store.

And while he might say he's meeting Vito, Angelo, Sal, and Paulie, the truth is he's probably meeting Vicky, Angelina, Sally, and Pauline. His Day Planner isn't going to say it, but the goomba could be setting up a date, arranging to purchase a bunch of stolen DVD players, placing a bet with his bookie, or, maybe, just going out for drinks and dinner.

But there are occasions in the goomba's life that are truly special occasions. Some of them are romantic special occasions.

Valentine's Day is a very big deal for the goomba. He's a sentimental guy. He likes to show off a little. He doesn't mind throwing a couple of bucks around to show how much he cares. So when

Another engagement party: good clean fun.

February 14 comes around, the goomba goes to town. But the goomba is a very social person, and he's more social than he is romantic. So he and his wife or his girl are going to celebrate with other couples. No other ethnic group does this, I'm sure, but Valentine's Day in the goomba world is a group holiday. The goomba celebrates Valentine's Day in a pack. And this is no romantic candlelight dinner at home. This is no intimate room service dinner in a hotel. Not for the goomba.

For the goomba, Valentine's Day is a big evening in a fancy restaurant at a table for twenty. There's going to be ten couples together for dinner. Or, even better, it's ten couples for an entire evening of Valentine's Day celebration. The goomba will book spaces at one of those big roadside hotels in New Jersey. He'll reserve the package. For $200, you get drinks and dinner and dancing, with a DJ, in the lounge, and then you get the room. I had eight couples, all friends of mine, who celebrated Valentine's Day this way just this year.

How romantic is that? The girls talk to the girls, and the guys talk to the guys. Just like Friday nights. Just like the night that a lot of these guys and girls met for the first time. Like their first dates. Like the night they fell in love. Everybody's happy.

That's not all, of course. The smart goomba has already bought the flowers, too. If the goomba is doing pretty good, he's going to the florist and arranging for something fancy to be delivered. If the goomba is having hard times, he's going to the corner market for a dozen roses on special for $9.99. (If the goomba really has it rough, or he's just a cheap bastard, he's going down to the guy on the corner and buy some wilted carnations for a couple of bucks.)

Either way, the evening is going to end with a toast of pink champagne, and a pink-colored, heart-shaped dessert. Well, that's not quite where it ends, but that's the last part that happens in public.

Among the non-goomba population, I've heard, Valentine's Day is a big time for marriage proposals. Lots of non-goombas go down on their knees and pop the big question, somewhere after the chocolate and flowers but before the Victoria's Secret.

Not in the goomba world. In the goomba world, the goomba always pops the question on Christmas Eve. I don't know why this is. Maybe it's just laziness. The goomba knows all the family is going to be around. All the relatives are going to be in town. Everyone he's got to meet, everyone he's got to speak to, everyone he wants his girl to show off her ring to—they're here already. On Christmas Day, he's going to see her family, she's going to see his family, and everyone gets to hear the news and get excited and see the ring and say *"Salute!"*

A lot of goombas know, going in, what kind of engagement ring to buy. This is because the goomba-ette isn't shy about telling the goomba what kind of engagement ring to buy. She's pointed at rings in shop windows. She's pointed at rings on other girls' fingers. She says, "Don't you buy me some cheap junk like that," or, "If you don't bring home a diamond bigger than that, don't even bother asking." So he knows. She wants a 2.5 carat, Marquis-cut, platinum-band, whatever, or she ain't coming along.

A lot of goombas will speak to the family first. The goomba may go to the prospective father-in-law and ask for his blessing. He'll say all the usual stuff—I love your daughter, I will be a good husband and provider for her, I will take care of her forever, all that. Then he'll speak to the mother and the rest of the family.

Remember, he already knows all these people. Very few goombas get engaged to a girl they don't know very very well. She's a neighborhood girl. He went to school with her brothers. His father went to school with her father. Their mothers shop together and play cards every Thursday. So it's not like anyone's got to get acquainted here. They're already acquainted.

And it's not like it's going to be some big surprise. The goomba engagement is a long engagement, and it can take a long time to even get to the engagement. The goomba and the goomba-ette have been dating since high school. They've been going steady. They've been out, once a week, in the company of ten other goomba couples, for several years. No one's going to have a heart attack when they hear these two are engaged.

Still, you got to do it right. So the goomba pops the question on Christmas Eve. Then, on Christmas Day, he and his fiancée go around and get congratulated. The tradition says that the two families are going to be together to celebrate the happy news. All of this happens, by the way, with coffee and cookies. The whole thing is done with coffee and cookies. Without the coffee and cookies, no one could get engaged. Everybody's got to have an espresso and an anisette cookie, with maybe a little glass of Sambucca.

I've also heard of non-goombas getting married on Valentine's Day. That won't happen to the goomba. For one thing, it's too soon. You get engaged on Christmas Eve, you can't get married less than two months later. It's too short an engagement. Everyone will think the girl is pregnant. You can't have them thinking that about your wife.

Also, Valentine's Day comes in February. It's cold and wet and icy in goomba-land. Who wants to get married on a day like that? You want to wait for spring or summer, when it's nice out.

Also, Valentine's Day doesn't always fall on a Saturday or a Sunday. And the goomba can only get married on a Saturday or Sunday. Because that is when all the guests can come. Remember the goomba family is a working-class family, in most cases. They're not self-employed. They don't work at home. They've got jobs. They can't just call the boss and say they're not coming in because they've got a wedding in the middle of the week.

Besides that, there isn't enough time to make the arrangements. It might take a year, or even more, for the goomba-ette to line up the hall, the photographer, the DJ, the band, and the caterer she wants. These things are in high demand in the goomba world. Many of them are booked at least a year in advance. So getting engaged at Christmas and married in February wouldn't work.

MORE GOOMBA PERSONAL ADS

AGE: I could tell you—but I'd have to kill you.

OCCUPATION: I do things for a guy.

LAST GREAT BOOK I READ: That thing with the cat. In the hat.

FAVORITE ON-SCREEN SEX SCENE: The Pizza Man scene in *Debbie Does Brooklyn.*

BEST LIE I EVER TOLD: When I said "I do."

IN MY BEDROOM YOU'LL FIND: Bread crumbs.

CELEBRITY I MOST RESEMBLE: Mario the Plumber, from "Donkey Kong."

With everything that's been said so far, you might think the average goomba is a crass, vulgar, selfish pig when it comes to love. Unfortunately, you'd be right. The goomba is a man, and a lot of the time he's a real man—no apologies, no explanations. He knows what he wants, and he speaks his mind, and sometimes that comes off a little crude.

But the goomba is also a very romantic guy. Walking down the street, he may see a good-looking woman and say, "That's a nice piece of meat." But what he's really saying, deep down inside, is, "I'm so alone." He may tell a friend, "I'd sure like to get in there." But what he really means is, "My heart is breaking." He may tell himself, "I would cut off my right arm for ten minutes alone with that *puttana.*" But his heart tells him, "I'm in love!"

A lot of goombas are very sensitive, emotional men. They get choked up watching those Hallmark TV movies, and those AT&T long-distance TV commercials. They all have their favorite romantic films.

Romantic Goomba Movies
The Way We Was
The Bridges of Bergen County
Sleepless in Staten Island
. . . When Rocco Met Angie

It's not just movies. Goombas like mood music, too.

Romantic Goomba Songs
"I Will Always Love Youse"
"Killing Me Softly . . . with Piano Wire"
"The Lady in Red (Sauce)"
"You Take My (Garlic) Breath Away"

Around the holidays, there's even . . .

Romantic Goomba Christmas Songs
"I Saw Daddy Whacking Santa Claus"
"I'm Dreaming of a White Clam Sauce"
"I'll Be Home for Christmas (with Time Off for Good Behavior)"

VERBAL BLUNDERS

AS MUCH as he might practice, though, the goomba is no silver-tongued devil. For as many times as he says something smooth and suave, there's times when he really puts his foot in his mouth.

I was with these four guys from *The Sopranos* recently, in Atlantic City. We had a promotional engagement down there. We were eating dinner in this little restaurant. It was a small place. We were practically sitting on top of this other table with a girl and a guy in a goatee. The guy is checking us out. His girl is checking us out. And we're checking *her* out, on the sly.

After he gets his check, the guy in the goatee finally leans over and starts talking. He says, "I'm sorry to interrupt, but I have to tell you how much I like the show. I *love The Sopranos.*"

We thank the guy, but he's not done.

"It's true. I can't stand it when *The Sopranos* goes off the air. I don't know what to do with my Sunday nights."

That's too much for me. I look straight at this guy's girl, and I say, "Really? I can think of a few things to do on a Sunday night, I can tell you that."

The girl blushes. She looks at the guy with the goatee. Then she looks at me and says, "Um, that's my dad."

I wanted to die.

One time, when I was a maitre d' in Las Vegas, this party of six came in. And one of the broads was really messed up. She was stumbling and falling down. She could hardly hold her head up. I said to the guy that looked like her date, "Wait a minute, pal. What is this broad *on?*"

The lady standing behind her said, "She has cerebral palsy, you asshole."

I wanted to die.

Another time, when I was entertainment director for the Riviera, I booked the Shangri-Las—you know, the girl group that did "The Leader of the Pack." I'm talking to their manager on the phone. I tell him I need some color photographs of the act, for advertising. He says he doesn't have any. I tell him I need the pictures to promote the act. He says he doesn't have any. He's the manager! I'm getting aggravated with the guy. So I say, "Are you telling me that none of these three fucking twats has a fucking colored picture of the band?"

He says, "That's what I'm telling you. And I'm married to one of the three fucking twats."

I wanted to die.

Something like that happened to this goomba comedian I know. We were watching this lounge act, a black singer named Tomato. She's huge. Like, 350 pounds huge. Singing her ass off. We're standing next to the sound booth, along with the sound engineer and some skinny little white guy.

The comedian is mouthing off. He says, "Would you look at the fat ass on that broad? Look at the tits on her—they're bigger than my car!"

The skinny little white guy says, "Excuse me, sir, but that's my wife."

The comedian turned and walked away. A few minutes later, he came over to me and said, "I feel terrible. What should I do?"

I said, "Nothing. You can't take it back. You can't even apologize. Just take the hit and keep moving."

THE LITTLE EXTRAS

IF HE'S GOING on a date, and it's not Valentine's Day or Christmas Eve, the goomba's not going to have to sweat that many details. But if it's a special occasion, he's going to be trying to make sure everything is just right.

The choice of music can be important. The goomba is going to give that some thought. He's going to go through the vinyl, or the CDs, and pick out a few that will create the right atmosphere. He's going to get creative here. He's going to make the music reassuring and predictable, but he's going to throw in a few surprises.

I know one guy who only plays Johnny Mathis records when he thinks he's going to get laid. He puts the CDs on—like, five of them—and has them all poised and ready to go. When he gets the girl back to the apartment, he clicks on the CD player, and it's "Misty" and "Chances Are" for the next several hours.

But there are limits. There ain't going to be no rap. Rap music is not romantic music. Even if you like rap music—and it's possible there are people who do—it's not music to get laid by.

This is especially true of the goomba. He's probably not listening to much rap or hip hop, no matter what he's doing. Rap ain't goomba. First of all, it's the wrong ethnic groups. You see black rappers, and white rappers, and even Latino rappers, from Mexico and Cuba. You don't see any goomba rappers. So far, there are no Italian-American rappers out there that I know of.

If there were, you could spot them from their goomba names.

They'd be called stuff like "50 Large," or "Phat Phuk." They'd have names like "Grand Master XXL." Not Mac Daddy, but Macaroni.

They're not going on the menu for tonight. The goomba is going to lay out some Sinatra, maybe a little Dean Martin, and maybe a little Barry White. It's going to be "Strangers in the Night" and "Can't Get Enough of Your Love, Babe"—with a little "That's Amore" in between.

If he lives alone, the goomba is going to spend a few minutes cleaning up his apartment. He's going to take the dirty socks and underwear off the floor and shove them into the back of his closet. He's going to clean out the ashtrays and throw away the beer empties and toss out last week's pizza cardboards. The dirty magazines that Patty Bo and Puddy were looking at go back in the drawer with the porno videos. If the girl is really something special, the goomba's going to wash the dishes and spray a little air freshener around the place.

But remember that many goombas live at home until they get married. So the average goomba is probably going to tell his mother he's going out. She'll ask him who with. He'll tell her with his girlfriend. She'll tell him to be careful—and remind him not to get the girl pregnant. The goomba could be 40 years old, and his mother would still say this.

Or worse. I know a guy whose father used to say to him, "For God's sake, use protection! You're too young to have children. Don't let happen to you what happened to me and your mother!"

If they're going out, like I already said, the goomba is going to spend some time on the car. He's going to have it washed. He's going to Armor All the tires and the dashboard. He's going to hang a new pine-scented cardboard Christmas Tree from the rearview mirror.

Maybe he's made dinner reservations. Maybe he's having something delivered. Either way, you know there's going to be a meal. Nothing important ever happens in a goomba's life without food being part of it, and the romantic evening is no exception.

If it's just a date, the goomba is going to take the girl to his favorite place in the neighborhood. He wants to show the girl off to his friends. He wants to show the girl that he *has* friends. He's not going there to hang out, but he wants people to see her.

If it's a special date—like, if he thinks tonight is the night she's going to give it up—the goomba is going to take the girl to a special place. It might be a more expensive place in the neighborhood. It's not Vinnie's Pizzeria. It's not Casa D'Calzone. It's for sure not the Olive Garden. It's going to be something fancier and more formal. Linen tablecloths. Candles. A good wine list.

Frank and Mike with a hooker. Just kidding.

If it's an anniversary, the goomba's taking his girl to the place they met. Or the place they got engaged. The goomba may not like routine, but he likes tradition. So he's going to return to this special place, year after year. He and his goomba-ette are going to order the same thing they ordered "that night." God forbid the goomba ordered something he didn't like. He's going to have to eat that meal again one night every year for the next fifty years, like it or not. The goomba and his girl are going to talk about the same things they talked about the first night. They'll stroll down memory lane. Very sweet, the goomba and his goomba-ette.

There will be the same music playing in the restaurant as the goomba has already picked out at home. Or there might be something special, like a couple of violin players roaming around, or a singer, even, taking requests at the table and singing everyone's favorite song. You better hope not, 'cause you're going to hear "Volare" or "Everybody Loves Somebody" or "Strangers in the Night" fourteen times over the next two hours.

If it's a really *special* special evening, the goomba is wearing a necktie. But this is only if he's going out or doing something where that is required. In my father's time, you'd see the goombas going out to the Copa, or Toots Shor's, and they'd be dressed to the nines with the silk suits and the shirts with the long collars and the cashmere overcoats. Later, you'd see guys like "The Dapper Don," John Gotti, dolled up like some kind of fashion plate. For the average goomba, that day has passed. A lot of today's goombas only put on a necktie if they're on the way to the mortuary—either in the casket or going to view the casket.

It's like that joke. What do you call a goomba in a suit and tie? The defendant.

He's probably going to be wearing something more like a sweater with a sports coat. Or a nice shirt with a sports coat. The three-piece suit ain't happening for the goomba anymore.

Vincent Curatola, who plays Johnny Sack on *The Sopranos,* for example, got kind of mixed up recently when he had to dress up. It was one of those awards shows. We were all walking down the red carpet. The cameras were going and the flashbulbs were going and the reporters were standing there with their microphones.

Then Joan Rivers runs up to Vincent and says, "Whose suit are you wearing?"

He said, "Whatta you mean?"

She said, "Whose suit is it?"

He said, "Whatta you talking about? It's *my* suit."

She said, "No! I mean, who designed it?"

He said, "How the fuck should I know? It's from Men's Warehouse."

On the personal grooming front, the goomba has taken care of business here, too. Maybe he's been out to the barber shop for a haircut. Maybe he's gone the extra mile and had a manicure. He's done what he can to contain the excess hair—clipped the nose hairs, shaved his ears, trimmed the mat on his chest so it doesn't come up over his collar, maybe had someone run a lawn mower up and down his back . . . No. Not that last part. But he's done what he can to bring the fur down a notch.

He's showered and shaved. He's splashed on four or five ounces of Paco Rabanne or Aramis cologne. He's probably had a shoe shine. (The goomba does not shine his own shoes, by the way. That's a weird WASP thing, having that box of shoe shine equipment at home and spending Saturday afternoon buffing up the shoe leather. The goomba will spend an entire day polishing his car, but he won't polish his shoes. That's something you get the guy on the corner or the guy in Penn Station to do for you, for a couple of bucks and a tip. Polishing your own shoes would be like changing your own oil. There's something demeaning about it. The goomba don't like to get his fingers dirty.) When it's time to get dressed for the special occasion, some goombas will put on special clothing. One guy I know puts on a pair of bright red briefs. Maybe it's a really nice gold chain. Maybe it's the expensive aftershave.

Now he's ready for goomba love.

If the evening is special enough, like a birthday or an anniversary, the goomba might have planned some special entertainment. He might have bought tickets for a show. If he's really crazy about the girl, he might even suffer through something like *Cats* or

Mamma Mia. He might go to a movie, but his first choice is not going to be *The Hours* or *Bridget Jones' Diary.*

It's not because the goomba isn't emotional. He cries several times watching *The Godfather.* He knows every nuance of Al Pacino in *Scarface* and *Serpico.* When the two brothers played by Robert De Niro and Joe Pesci fight and yell in *Raging Bull,* it tears him up inside.

But there's a limit. He's a grown man. That means no kid stuff *(Mary Poppins, The Sound of Music)* unless he's with his kids, and no chick flicks *(Terms of Endearment, Beaches)*—unless he's trying really hard to get laid.

The goomba ain't gonna sit still for *Bridges of Madison County, Dirty Dancing, Sleepless in Seattle, The Wedding Planner,* or *What Women Want.* Because, really, who cares what women want? Not the goomba. It's Valentine's Day, but let's be realistic. The very most you can expect of him is, say, *Moonstruck.* At least it's about Italians.

If goombas ran Hollywood, this would all be different. The movies would all be about Italian-American guys facing terrible struggles and coming out on top. Every movie would be *Rocky,* basically, and tell the story of a guy whose last name is something like Balboa.

And the chick flicks would come out pretty different, too. *Pretty Woman* is about a hooker who meets a rich man and turns into a nice girl. What a load! All that happens to hooker who meets a rich man is she turns into a *retired* hooker. She's still a *whoo-ah.*

All the TV shows would be different, too. If you look at prime-time TV today, most of that is crap the average goomba can't bear to watch. He's into *Everybody Loves Raymond,* because Ray Romano is one of us and he seems like a guy you'd like to hang out with. He's watching *The Sopranos,* of course, because it is basically the best show that was ever on TV. He's checking out George Lopez's show and Damon Wayans's show because he can watch with his kids and deep down both guys are goombas at heart.

If it was up to him, the goomba would take all the rest of the stuff on TV and turn it into something he could watch. There wouldn't be any *Friends,* unless it was about five guys from Canarsie. There wouldn't be any *Frasier,* unless it was called *Frascati* and it was about a sanitation worker from New Jersey. And, believe me, all those cop shows would end very differently. The good guy would be the bad guy, and the bad guy would always get away.

If the goomba ran the network programming, your *TV Guide* would look like this:

I Love Luigi
Fresh Prince of Bensonhurst
All My Chianti
Who's the (Mob) Boss?
Monday Night Football
Tuesday Night Football
Wednesday Night Football
Rocco's Modern Life
America's Funniest Surveillance Videos
Who Wants to Whack a Millionaire?
Molto Mario (because that guy is great)

There would be special channels, too. You could watch MSTV, which would be Martin Scorsese television, with Scorsese movies all day and night. VH-1 and MTV, those would have to go. Some of those other channels—BET, Lifetime, Oxygen—I don't think we'd be keeping those, either. Some shows—*Touched by an Angel,* for example—*fuhgeddaboudit.*

There are also, of course, romantic goomba books.

Just kidding.

This is a sensitive area, but another goomba special occasion is the bachelor party.

Not all goombas have one. I didn't have one. But it's kind of a tradition in the world I grew up in. And I've been to plenty of them.

Traditionally, all the goomba pals have to take the goomba who's getting married out on the town for one last fling with his bachelorhood. Remember, we're talking old-fashioned Italian-American goombas, here. This guy ain't walking down the aisle with some chick he met last week at the track. And he ain't planning to give it a year or two and see if it works out. This is *for life.*

A goomba engagement party. A hand in your crotch is better than one in your pocket.

He's known this girl for years. He knows her father and mother and brothers and sisters. He knows her grandparents. And everyone he knows, they know all those people too. He's going to move into a new place in the neighborhood and be surrounded *for life* by these people.

In other words, he may not have much fooling around in his future.

So the boys have to take him out for one last wild night.

The boys have made some arrangements. These depend on the economic circumstances of the group. If it's a middle-class group, and everyone is doing okay, there's going to be a nice Italian meal in a neighborhood restaurant. There's going to be lots of wine and food and singing and joking.

Afterwards, the guys are all driving to a strip joint. There's going to be more drinking and joking and singing. And maybe a little fooling around, if they get lucky.

When you think of it that way, it's kind of charming, isn't it?

And after that there might be something else.

If they guys have a little less dough, they don't go to a strip joint. Instead, they have a stripper come to a cheap hotel room. There's going to be more drinking and joking, and definitely some fooling around.

And after that there might be something else.

I don't want to necessarily say what the something else is. One of the rules of the bachelor party is you don't say what goes on there. You don't want the new bride to know where her new husband was the night before they got married.

Of course sometimes there's no avoiding that. Some goomba-ettes are more or less aware of what goes on at these bachelor parties. And every once in a while there is some hen-pecked *mamaluke* of a guy who tells his wife or his girlfriend what happened at his friend Angelo's bachelor party—just so he can assure his wife or girlfriend that he, the *mamaluke*, didn't participate in any of that.

Plus, it has to be said, occasionally there has been the unlucky new husband who has taken something on his honeymoon that he got at the bachelor party. Many's the goomba who has had to try to think of a way to explain to his new bride why she has to take penicillin, too, because of the cold he's got. Or has to explain to her why, even though they're married, they should wait to have sex until they're settled into their new home. Or whatever. This goomba is scrambling. He'll make up anything at this point rather than tell the truth.

Because the truth, it's not all that pretty. Just for the sake of illustration, let's imagine a goomba bachelor party. Not that I've ever seen anything exactly like this, but just imagine it.

After the stripper has done her stripping, many a time she will stay on to do a little extra. There's money flying around. There's some guys with their pants off. There's a back room with a bed in it, and pretty soon one of the guys is throwing out a little extra money and taking the stripper into that back room. Pretty soon, he isn't the only one. Maybe half the guys take their turn. And, in a lot of these situations, a collection is taken to make sure the groom gets a turn, too, without having to pay for it.

There's no shame in any of this. There is no disrespect to the bride—even though this is all happening the week before or even the night before her wedding. In fact, in many circumstances, the groom will invite his brothers-in-law-to-be to the bachelor party. And they will partake right along with the rest of the guys.

I have even known of situations where the prospective father-in-law attends the bachelor party. I remember one time when the father of the bride-to-be was getting blown by the hooker, right alongside his future son-in-law.

The modern goomba, these days, makes an excursion out of it. The guys will rent a Winnebago and have someone drive them down to Atlantic City. They'll drink and gamble and get a stripper or a hooker to come back to the Winnebago and do the dirty deed right there. Or they'll get a big suite in a hotel, in Las Vegas, and have a wild party up there.

Either way, the point is the same. The goomba's wild days are over. He's going to settle down and become a family man now. He's going to be responsible. He's going to be an adult. So, he needs one last opportunity to act like an animal. And, like every other important moment in a goomba's life, he wants to do it in the company of the ones he loves best. He needs his friends along for the ride.

*Material Love: The
Things a Goomba
Can't Resist*

*. . . it's important
to know if you're
in a car that belongs to
a goomba who's going
to freak out if you
smudge the windows.*

$\mathcal{T}$he goomba is just a big kid, in a lot of ways. He likes the nice stuff in life. And, being a goomba, what he loves, he loves *a lot*. The goomba doesn't like macaroni. He loves it! He doesn't just like his car. He loves his car! And his music. And his favorite restaurant. And his favorite sports team. And his clothes. And his jewelry. And everything else that matters to him. These may be inanimate things to some guys. To the goomba, these are the stuff that dreams are made of.

The average goomba, especially the young goomba, loves his car more than anything else in his life. This is how they spend their Saturday. They have a whole ritual. They get out there in the drive-way, in their jogging suits—not the good jogging suit, just the reg-ular Saturday afternoon jogging suit—and they spend three or four hours washing and waxing the thing. They do the windows. They take a break and have a sandwich. They replace the air freshener. They do the rims and the tires. They polish up the special writing on the back. I had one friend whose Camaro said, "Crystal Blue Persuasion." A lot of goombas would have their names pin-striped on the door, right under the door handle. Sometimes they'd have their girlfriend's name written in the same place on the passenger door. I had one friend who had his girlfriend's name—Monica—written on one side, and his own name—Angelo—on the other.

A goomba and his Caddy. Is there any more love than this?

Then he broke up with the girlfriend. New paint job! Some guys have the horn that plays the theme song from *The Godfather.*

I know a goomba in Las Vegas who drives an $85,000 Mercedes. Nothing strange in that, right? But he lives in a $30,000 mobile home! This is goomba car obsession taken to an unhealthy extreme, but it's not all that weird. It's just a goomba with different priorities.

My friend Richie was a bit of a nut about his car. In 1976 he had a brand new Monte Carlo. White. Bucket seats. Landau top. It was very sharp, and he was obsessed with keeping it sharp. I think he washed the car every single day. He was a little vain, maybe—because he had his own initials pin-striped on the doors on both sides. The car had huge speakers in it, and some kind of jewelry hanging from the rearview mirror. That car was our ride. We'd go out and cruise around, some nights, up and down 86th Street, with disco music blasting, checking everything out.

Another one of our guys, Larry, he had a brand new

Thunderbird. It was jet black. Which meant every speck of dirt showed up. He'd have to walk around the car every half an hour or so, looking for dust. He's see a fingerprint or a smudge on the door and have to take the sleeve of his shirt and start rubbing it out. And he was like Richie. He didn't trust the car wash not to put scratches in the car. So several times a week he'd wash the car himself, by hand, in his driveway. Sometimes we'd crack open the fire hydrant and fill a bucket, and wash the car right on the street corner.

Goombas, because of the strong feeling they have for their cars, are very protective of their cars. So it's important to know if you're in a car that belongs to a goomba who's going to freak out if you smudge the windows.

HOW TO TELL IF YOU'RE IN A GOOMBAMOBILE

There's an air freshener and a giant plastic pepper hanging from the rearview mirror.

There's a statue of St. Anthony on the dashboard, holding a Giants pennant.

There's pizza crusts under the front seat.

There's a baseball bat under the other front seat.

The windows are tinted. And bullet-proof.

Some guys had strict rules. You can't eat in the car. Or smoke in it. Or put your feet on the seats. Or your hands on the windows. Mess up, and you're gonna get a beating. You've seen those stupid bumper stickers that say, "You toucha my car, I breaka you face"? No real goomba would have that on the car. That would be stupid. You don't warn someone. You just break their face.

It's not just a point of pride with these guys. The car is a very important thing. Lots of young goombas live at home. So this car, it's more than a car. It's a bedroom. It's the little love nest. This is where they take the girls, when they take 'em out. So, you know, it's gotta be nice.

I used to have a friend from the neighborhood that drove a '65 Mustang. Cherry. Beautiful. And he doted on the car the way some people dote on their children. He drove it everywhere. But he couldn't leave it alone. He'd come to a party, and park the car on the street—after first driving around to find a parking place where no one was going to open a door into it and nick the paint job. Then he'd come inside the party. But after about two minutes he'd say, "I'm just going to check on the car." If you looked out the window, you'd see him standing there wiping dust off the hood with his handkerchief.

One time he offered to take me for a ride. I was pretty excited. He didn't take anybody for a ride. I started to get in, but he said, "Hey! Hold on! The shoes." He made me take off my shoes before I got into the car. He said, "Sorry, man. I just got new floor mats."

GOOMBAS LOOKING SHARP

SOME GOOMBAS are slobs. But some goombas are very fussy about their clothes. Looking good is very important. Some guys get obsessive about it. It may look to you like the goomba is just wearing a track suit. But he might have spent quite a lot of time picking out that track suit. He might have a dozen just like it, in different shades or colors. He might have spent quite a lot of time deciding which pair of shiny black shoes go best with that track suit.

In other words, the goomba might be a snappy dresser or he might dress like a slob. But there are some general rules about goombas and clothes.

Things the goomba will never wear
- ♥ smoking jacket
- ♥ A derby
- ♥ A baseball cap—turned backwards
- ♥ An ascot
- ♥ Ear muffs
- ♥ Spandex
- ♥ Plaid
- ♥ A fez
- ♥ A Stetson
- ♥ Chaps and spurs

The goomba is going to buy most of his clothing from a neighborhood shop. He wants to shop where he's comfortable. He's not going to Saks or Bloomingdales. He'll buy a suit and some shirts from a shop around the corner. If he's a fat goomba, like me, he's going to go to Rochester Big and Tall. That's where all the fat guys go. They've even got pictures of famous fat guys on the wall—Al Roker, John Madden, John Goodman. Last time I was there, they offered to put my picture on the wall, too. I said, "That's not a wall of fame I want to be on."

Unlike some non-goomba guys, the goomba is not going to buy clothes from a catalog. He's not going to buy from a big-name company either. That stuff's too fancy, and it's always got someone else's name on it somewhere. The goomba isn't into the logo thing. So he's not doing the Ralph Lauren Polo thing. And he's not shopping the WASP labels either. No Abercrombie and Fitch. No L.L. Bean. No Brooks Brothers.

But the goomba can be quite serious about what he wears. Some goombas get carried away. My friend Mike has an uncle who can't wear any piece of new clothing until he has written his name, the date, and the name of the shop where he bought the clothing—

Johnny in a cheap motel in a cheap white suit.

on the clothing. He writes all this stuff right on the tag of a new shirt, or a new suit, or a new pair of pants. He even writes it in his shoes. That way, if something goes wrong, he can take the shoes back and complain. He *could* just save the receipt. But this guy's old school. He writes it right in the shoe. He's the kind of goomba that I used to see at the beach, when I was a kid. He'd be wearing bathing trunks with the matching jacket and the matching hat.

Other guys are obsessive even though they don't dress up. I know one guy, a goomba from Canarsie, who irons his jeans. Even if he's just going down to the corner market, wearing jeans and a T-shirt, he's got to wear perfectly pressed jeans and a T-shirt. If the jeans are wrinkled, he won't wear them.

Some of this comes from when we grew up. It was the disco period, in the 1970s. All us goombas wore the doubleknit pants and the polyester shirts, and some guys even had one of those *Saturday Night Fever* suits. Most of us didn't go that far. My friend Richie owned two shirts and two pair of pants. The gray pants went with the black shirt, and the black pants went with the gray shirt. That was it. He used to say, "One's for Friday night, and one's for Saturday night." Bingo. He was covered.

His brother used to iron the collars of his shirts, too. He'd starch these giant collars and make them stand up like they had rigor mortis. That was the look. Like the rest of us, he'd spend about an hour blow-drying his hair, pushing it straight back and out to the sides, until it was perfect. Some guys used hair spray, even, to make sure the hair stayed just right for the rest of the evening.

A lot of this was wiseguy stuff. Not that everyone was a wiseguy. And not that everyone used that terminology. In fact, some goombas I know never used that word, even. They wouldn't say, "He's a wiseguy," or "He's a goodfella." They would only say, "He's good people."

And even if they were afraid of these guys, they admired them, too. My friends Mike and Frank remember that Vito Genovese used to come into their neighborhood. When they'd leave, he'd throw a handful of quarters and half-dollars up in the air for the neighborhood kids to grab. That made an impression.

In those days, being Italian wasn't so cool. I remember some of the older men talking about how the Irish cops used to refer to Italians as "white niggers." That's pretty hard, growing up in that environment. So anybody that had money, that dressed nice, that didn't look afraid . . . You looked up to that. And the wiseguys always had the best cars and the best clothes and looked like they had money to burn. Some goombas, today, are still going for that all-out, high-class look.

GAMBLING GOOMBAS

THE AVERAGE GOOMBA doesn't have a hobby. That's a WASP thing, I think. Your goomba ain't collecting no stamps. He ain't chasing butterflies or watching birds. He's not much of an athlete, so all that tennis and golf stuff is out. He ain't jogging, or running, unless it's from the cops. For the goomba, hobbies would be eating, screaming, and scratching his balls.

The closest thing to a true goomba hobby is probably gambling.

Most goombas gamble at one time or another. I don't care where they come from, where they live, what they do for a living, whether they're rich or poor, whether they're mobbed up or not. All goombas love gambling. And all goombas gamble, one way or another.

I'm not just saying this because I live in Las Vegas. I knew about goombas and gambling long before I ever heard of Las Vegas. My father was a gambler and a bookmaker. He was working both sides of it. He'd make some bets, and he'd take some bets. And everyone in the neighborhood where I grew up was involved in some kind of legal or illegal gambling. They were betting on the horses, or the basketball game, or the football game, or the fights. They were playing the numbers. They were involved in illegal poker or craps games. Even the old women played cards for penny-a-point stakes. It's in the blood.

And it's a whole universe that most outsiders don't understand.

My friend Joe told me he started gambling in the fourth grade. He would sneak off every day and pitch nickels against this urine-stained staircase at the back of the school, playing against the black guys in the school. I asked him what in the world was so attractive about pitching nickels against some piss-stinking stairs with a bunch of guys he didn't know. He said, "I don't know. I just loved the action."

I was a teenager before I really got involved with it. Then I started betting on the ball games. I'd get together with the guys on Saturday. We'd argue and yell about the game on Sunday or the game on Monday. Whether it was basketball or football, we'd argue about it. Then we'd decide how much money we were going to lay down, on which team. Then we'd call the bookie.

Everybody knew a bookie. Most people who gambled a lot knew several bookies. Someone would introduce you. Someone would "vouch" for you. After that, you'd get a phone number and you'd be able to make the call.

So we'd get the bookie on the phone and we'd all place our bets. You'd say something like, "Yeah, it's Steve. Gimme the Giants ten times."

That meant you were going to bet $50 that the Giants were going to win. Each "time" was $5. So "five times" was $25, "ten times" was $50, and so on.

Some guys would lay down several bets. There might be a basketball game Sunday and a football game Monday night. You'd lay them out there. Five on this, ten on that.

The bookie would take the bet. We'd go back to arguing and yelling. The next day, we'd get together and watch the game, and then we'd all argue and yell after we won and lost.

Then it was time to settle up. If you had bet the Giants ten times, and the Giants won, the bookie owed you $50. If you bet the Giants ten times and the Giants lost, you owed the bookie $50 plus the $5 "vig," or "vigorish." That was like the interest on the bet. Or the price of him taking the bet.

Depending on how you did, you'd either settle up on the phone or you'd have to go see the bookie in person. If you won, you might leave the money as a kind of credit. The next week, you could do the Giants twenty times, with the money you made last week. Or you could make two bets with the $100.

If you lost, you probably had to go see the guy in person. He'd work out of a restaurant, or one of the social clubs. Or sometimes he'd have a legitimate business. He'd run a laundry or a dry cleaners or a barber shop. You'd go in and make good. That way, next week, you could call him and make another bet.

In the old days, all of the guys I knew used the same bookie. He ran a candy store, right in the neighborhood. When we wanted to place a bet, we called or we stopped by. When we won, or we lost, we went to the candy store to settle up.

Mr. Candy Store was doing well for himself. He always wore the most beautiful watches and the most expensive looking jewelry. And beautiful clothes, too. Especially for a candy store owner. He was making a lot of money, from the candy and the bookmaking. And either way our bets went, the bookie came up good.

That's because he had this huge inventory of stuff in the back room. He was selling candy. But he was selling a lot of stuff that just fell off the back of the truck, too. He had leather jackets and bottles of perfume and new silk shirts. So, if you lost, you lost and you had to pay up. But if you won, you'd get your money and then you'd have to do a little shopping. How about a nice sports coat? How about a leather jacket? He had us coming and going.

As long as you're betting and winning, or betting and losing and covering your bets, you're doing good. If you're losing and you can't cover your bets, you have a problem.

Most guys solve the problem the stupid way. You lost money on a bet. You can't pay the bookie for the bet. So, you get another bookie to take another bet. If you win that, you can pay the first bookie off, and still be almost even. Trouble is, some guys with gambling problems make dumb bets. Pretty soon, they owe money to several bookies. None of these guys will take his bet. He doesn't have any money. What's he going to do?

The bookie probably won't let him get too deep. He doesn't want a problem. He's in the betting business. Not in the collections business. He wants the guy to get straightened out and start betting again. So, he introduces the guy to a shylock.

A friend of mine who's been down this road many a time, with many a bookie, says the conversation usually goes like this. The gambler calls the bookie after he loses. The bookie says, "Here is your figure. When can I pick it up?"

And the gambler says, "I don't got it."

"What do you mean you don't got it?"

"I don't got it."

"Can you get it?"

"Not right away."

"Don't you know somebody?"

"No. Not for that kind of money."

"Okay. I know somebody. Give this guy a call."

Suddenly, the gambler knows somebody. He knows a shy.

The shylock isn't in the gambling business. He's in the lending business. If you've got some gambling debts, and some collateral of some kind, the shylock will be happy to help you consolidate your debts and get back on your feet. But he charges a hefty interest. You borrow some money, you agree on a weekly payment. At the very least, you make that interest payment. Then when your ship comes in, you pay off the whole thing.

Depending on how well you know the shy, or depending on who vouches for you to the shy, and whether you're a neighborhood guy or not, the vig is "a point," or it's "a point and a half." That means 10 or 15 percent interest, a week. If you borrow $1,000, you owe $100 a week.

And most shylocks won't take "knockdowns" or "knockdown payments." You can't pay off the debt $100 or $300 or $500 at a time. You have to come up with the entire $1,000, or keep paying that $100 a week.

That's the theory anyway. But I know guys who got into a shylock for five hundred, and who have been paying $50 a week on the vig. For years, I mean for *years*, they're paying that vig. They don't

touch the principal. Probably because they keep gambling, and losing. They can always find $50 to get the shylock off their back for
another week. But over time, boy does it add up. That $50 a week,
for a year, that's $2,600. And he still owes the shylock the original
five hundred!

If the guy starts missing the vig, then he's got trouble. The shylock ain't gonna wait around forever. He'll let you go a week, or a
few weeks, but sooner or later he's gonna send someone to talk to
you. At first, you're going to get slapped around. Then you're going
to get punched. Unlike what you've seen in the movies, these guys
usually don't kill you—because then they're not going to get their
money. But they may dangle you off a hotel balcony. They may do
something more violent, to send a message to the community that
they won't let anyone get away with borrowing money and not paying it back. You may get your leg broken, or your kneecaps shot off.

Or, if you own something of value, you may wind up with a new
business partner. Many's the goomba that got into trouble with
gambling, ran over his bookie, got hooked into a shylock, and
started to lose the family business. Suddenly Nino's Neopolitan
Pizzeria has a new partner, and he gets half of the weekly take.

Lots of guys use shylocks, by the way, even when they don't gamble at all. Shylocks are very handy for guys who need money for
things that the bank won't lend them money for. You can't go into
Citibank and say, "I need $10,000 for this shipment of stolen TVs."
You can't go into Bank of America and say, "I need a line of credit
real fast so I can move five kilos of heroin." So some guys use shylocks exclusively, no matter what their financial need.

In my experience, with what I've seen, there is nothing in the
world worse than gambling. Nothing will tear the goomba down
faster. It's worse than booze or drugs or women. I mean, whoever
you are, you can only drink so much. You can only do so much

cocaine. You'll quit drinking and drugging before the money runs out, unless you just die. But gambling is a bottomless pit. With gambling you can go on and on until there's nothing left.

That's what happened to my friend Joe Gannascoli, who's also known as Joe Soup. He had a gambling problem. It turned into a big problem. He got behind. He started owing some money. He got a little more behind. Pretty soon he was betting heavier, because he had heavy losses he was trying to cover. The $500 bet started turning into the $5,000 bet. One football season he see-sawed back and forth—he was up $5,000, he was down $7,000, he was up $10,000, he was down $12,000.

Then came the fateful Sunday. Joe had a pretty sure thing going with the Giants at New England. The Giants were going for the playoffs. New England was going nowhere. Joe had the Giants for $15,000. They lost, 12-10.

Joe bet heavy on the second game of the day, trying to make it up. He laid down $15,000 on a Jets game. It wasn't such a sure thing. And it didn't come in. By four o'clock in the afternoon, Joe was out $30,000—far, far more than he'd ever been down before.

So he did the natural thing. The Steelers and the Oilers were playing at eight o'clock. The Steelers were a lock to win. The season was almost over. The Oilers were playing their number two quarterback, a guy named Cody Carlson. Joe felt pretty safe with this bet. So he bet big. He phoned his bookie and took the Steelers for $30,000.

Carlson threw for 450 yards. The Oilers rolled over the Steelers. Joe was out $60,000. That was a Sunday night. By Friday, of the next week, he had sold his interest in his restaurant, liquidated his assets, paid off his bookie and his shy, and left town. He moved to California to revive his career as an actor—his true calling. Years later, he was cast as Vito on *The Sopranos*.

To this day, whenever he gets a good part, or whenever a show or a movie he's in gets a good review, he thanks Cody Carlson. But you can see him shudder when he talks about the 60 grand.

I asked him once how come he didn't just skip town, instead of paying off. If he was leaving for L.A. anyway, why didn't he just blow off the bookie and the shy and run for it?

Joe's a real goomba. He couldn't do that. He said, "That was not an option. I would have expected to get paid if I won. So I expected to pay if I lost. I knew I was ruined—I lost my restaurant, my girl, my family, everything. But skipping wasn't an option."

When I was younger, all the guys I knew liked to go to the track and bet on the horses. It was a nice way to spend an evening. Or an afternoon. I knew guys who'd call in sick and go spend the day at the track. Or guys that would tell their wives they were working late, and go to the track.

It was low-level stuff. We'd take a little money, enough to lay down a few bets and have a few beers, and go out in a group of eight or ten guys. We'd get a Racing Form and read the stuff like we knew what it meant. Sometimes somebody would get a tip, from a friend, or from a bookie, and we'd all lay down a bet. Or not. I remember one time this guy stopped us as we were going in and fed us a line about some horse. Only one guy in our group was stupid enough to go for it. And the horse came in at 35-to-1 or something.

When that happened, the guy that won was stuck for the rest of the week. Wherever we went, whatever we did, he was buying, until the money was gone. He'd have to buy all the drinks for the next week. That was just the rule. Everyone shared.

You can tell a lot about people from the way they gamble, too. The guys I know who work in casinos have slang words for different types of gamblers. A guy who really throws money around is a

"George." A guy who tips even bigger is a "King George." A guy who's got tons of money and bets big is a "whale." A guy who's got tons of money and bets big and tips big is a "King Kong."

The dealers know all the whales and all the King Kongs. If one of them is coming to town, the word will get out. Because when a whale comes into the place, everybody makes a little extra money.

Ben Affleck used to be known as a King Kong. All the casino guys loved him. He comes in and drinks and gambles and has a good time. He likes to laugh. He doesn't put on airs. And he's a huge tipper.

So is his pal Matt Damon, only not as often and not as big. So is George Clooney, only the same thing—he's a good guy, but he doesn't throw it around like Ben.

Or like Ben *used to*. Because all the casino guys feel differently about Ben now that he's with that Jennifer Lopez.

Here's why.

Ben came in one night with J. Lo. He was gambling. She was goofing around. She kept coming over to the table and trying to get him to quit playing blackjack and go shopping with her. Finally he did. So, the dealers are thinking, "What a *mamaluke!* The guy's got a ring in his nose!" But then he comes back and plays some more. And all the guys like him, because he's funny and he's one of the boys and he tips big.

This night, he's back into the blackjack when J. Lo comes around again and starts telling him she wants to leave. So, finally, he agrees to stop playing. He's been way up, and he's been way down, and he's had a lot of laughs, so he does the right thing. He takes a $5,000-chip and throws it on the table, and says, "Thanks, guys."

And J. Lo picks the chip up, *off the table,* and puts it in her purse. She says, "What are you doing? You don't need to leave that much."

And she puts $100 on the table and walks away.

As my friend Mike says, "That was it, with her. No one will ever look at her the same way again."

When a goomba comes to the table, the dealers recognize him right away. Some of them are really obnoxious. These are like the wiseguy wanna-bes. They pull out the big bankroll so everybody can see. They peel a few thousand off. They make a big deal out of making their bets. They throw two thousand bucks down like it was fifty cents. And they've got all this casino lingo. "Give me six bits on the four and ten." Two bits is a quarter, which means two bits can be $25. So that means, "Place $75 each on the four and the ten, please." They'll say, "Give me a bean on the five and nine." A bean is $100. They'll say, "Give me a mallard on the hard eight." A mallard is $50. Some of these guys are what my friend Mike calls "real guidos." These are the ones that come in talking that line, wearing the giant pinky ring and the gold chains, and the white leather shoes with the matching belt, and the girlfriend or the wife with the giant hair. He calls everybody *cugine,* which means "cousin" in Italian and is like a black guy calling another black guy "brother," or maybe "blood."

Most of the gambling I saw when I was younger was pretty innocent. That changed as I got older. I've seen people ruin themselves almost overnight with gambling since I moved out to Las Vegas. Most of them are perfectly nice people who did not have any gambling problem at all. Until they had a big gambling problem. Then they fell apart.

I know there's this idea that the locals don't gamble in Las Vegas. That's a load of crap. If the locals don't gamble, then why does every bar, every restaurant, every convenience store, and every laundromat have a video poker machine in it? And who are all those deadbeats sitting at the poker machines at 9:00 AM on a Wednesday morning—in the 7-Eleven? It's the locals, not tourists, and the locals get into just as much trouble with gambling as the tourists do. Bigger trouble, in fact, because they're not going back to Milwaukee on Sunday night with their tails between their legs. They're going to stay in town and keep losing until there's nothing left.

Not that all of them are losers. I know some guys who are professional gamblers. They get up in the morning—or in the afternoon, or in the evening, depending on what kind of guys they are—and shower and shave and go to work just like everyone else. Only their work is poker or blackjack. They take a little bankroll. They go to the casino. They sit at the table. They work, until they've made whatever their target amount is, and then they get up and leave. Maybe they need to make $300 a day. The good gamblers will play until the bankroll is gone, no matter how long that is, or until they've made their $300, no matter how long that is. If they hit it good and make $300 in two hours, they take the rest of the day off. If it takes ten hours to make the $300, they work a little unpaid overtime.

Then there are the ones who get wiped out.

I had a friend who came out here from New York with his wife. He wasn't much of a player, but she liked to gamble a little. She liked the slots. They'd come out on vacation two or three times a year. She'd play the slots. No big deal. But when they moved out here, suddenly she discovers the video poker machines. In the laundromat. She starts playing video poker, at the laundromat. Pretty soon she's playing all day long. And she's losing. When he came out to Las Vegas, my friend had about $80,000 in the bank. Before she was finished with the video poker, $65,000 of it was gone. His wife stopped right before the money was all gone.

I know another couple. He was a house painter from Buffalo. After a long career, he retires. He pays off the mortgage and sells the house. He and the wife used to come out to Las Vegas a few times a year. Now they've retired to Las Vegas. They've got a nest egg of about $150,000. They were going to buy a house and settle down. But they started gambling. For about three months, they acted like high rollers. At the end of three months, the money was all gone. My friend went back to house painting. His wife had to get a job working for minimum wage at a fast food restaurant. Ruined.

I'm lucky nothing like that happened to me. I learned my lesson the hard way, when I was kind of new in Las Vegas. Like I said, I used to place a few bets with a bookie when I was 19 or 20. By the time I'm 21, I'm living in Las Vegas. I've got a job making a few hundred a week. I'm paying $150 a month in rent, sharing with a couple of other guys. Life is good. I've got a little bankroll. I've got about $1,000 in cash. I'm going to open a bank account.

I'm with some guys at this casino. I've worked all night, the sun has just come up, and we're sitting having a few drinks. Some of the guys start throwing down a few bets. They're playing blackjack. I'm having a drink and watching.

And then, for some reason, I said, "Let me jump in here." I make a few bets. I make about $100. I have another drink or two. I make another couple of bets. Now I lose $100. And another $100. And another. I can't win a hand. So I do the usual stupid thing. I start doubling my bet.

And you can guess what happened. I lost almost all the money. In fact, I did lose all the money—all I had. At some point one of my friends made me give him $200 out of my bankroll. I lost all the rest. All $800.

I realize that doesn't seem like a lot of money. But it was all the money I had in the world. I had blown everything I had.

I wanted to cry for my mother. I felt so bad. I felt worse than I'd ever felt in my life. To me now it would be like losing everything—the house, the car, the clothes, everything! I wanted to cry like a baby.

But I was cured. After that, I never had a gambling thing again. These days, I go nuts and throw $100 down for the Super Bowl. My wife teases me. She's the only wife in America that picks on her husband for not betting enough. "What are you doing to do? A whole hundred? Whooooo . . . High roller!"

If you want some evidence that Las Vegas gambling isn't all fun and games, consider the fact that there are bookies all over the casinos. How could that be? Every casino has a sports book. You can walk in and place a bet on any sports event you like, and it's all aboveboard and perfectly legal. Why the hell would there be bookies around there? Because that way you can place a bet without laying down any money. You can make a bet with money you don't actually have. The casinos are very liberal, but they won't let you bet with money you don't have. The bookies will. So you can dig yourself into an even deeper hole.

SPORTY GOOMBAS

EVEN FOR GUYS who don't gamble, the average goomba really likes sports. Some of them like to play sports. Almost all of them like to watch sports. The average goomba is a real fan. If he's a Yankees fan, he's a die-hard Yankees fan. He may love the Mets. He may be a Jets fan or a Giants fan. Whatever the case, he's very loyal to the hometown team. And it's not just New York. There are no bigger baseball fans than the goombas who follow the Chicago Cubs.

Baseball is probably the number-one goomba sport. The goomba loves going to the ball game. There's nothing better than an evening at Yankee Stadium. You go with four or five guys, have a few beers, have a few hot dogs, sit outside on a warm summer night . . . beautiful. If you can't make it to the game, you watch it on TV. When I was a kid, and it was baseball season, every single TV in Brooklyn was tuned to the ball game. Guys were watching at home, at the social club, at the bar, at the corner store, in the pizzeria, everywhere. It was like the whole place just stopped.

One of the greatest things that happened to me last year was going to Yankee Stadium, with a bunch of people from *The Sopranos*, to throw out the first ball. It was a day before the season premiere of the show, and five of us went out, and stood there with five balls, and threw out the first ball of the game. There were 44,000 people in the stands. And we got to keep the balls! This is a goomba dream come true.

When I was a kid, a lot of the sports heroes were goomba ballplayers, and many of them came from Brooklyn. We loved to hear about guys like Joe DiMaggio, and Phil Rizzuto, and Yogi Berra. We loved Joe Pepitone, Lee Mazzilli, Bob Aspromonte, Sal Maggio, Al Ferrara, and Joe Garagiola. We even loved Sandy Koufax. He was Jewish, but he was from Brooklyn, and he was a Dodger. Later on, we all loved Joe Torre, the most goomba of all goomba ballplayers.

For those who play sports, too, there are pretty specific rules. Some sports are good for goombas, and some sports are not. For example:

The goomba isn't playing lacrosse or squash. That's for WASPS.

The goomba isn't playing Ping-Pong. That's for Chinese guys.

The goomba isn't playing hockey. That's for Canadians.

The goomba isn't into track and field events. If he's running, it's because he's running from a cop.

The goomba isn't playing badminton or croquet. That's for English guys. Plus, like soccer, these require large grassy areas.

The goomba isn't playing polo. A horse is something for a jockey to ride so the goomba can make a bet on it.

The goomba is, however, playing racquetball, and handball, and paddleball. Those are city games that you play on concrete or asphalt. Where I grew up, we even played softball on asphalt. It was like sandlot baseball, but on a hard surface like a school playground. The goomba is hunting and fishing, too. Even though these are not done on asphalt, they do involve killing stuff. And what guy doesn't like that?

FOOD—THE CENTER OF GOOMBA LIFE

OF COURSE EVERYONE knows that a goomba loves his food—and lots of it. I'm not saying this because I'm a big guy with a big appetite. I'm saying this because I'm a goomba. Food is what holds goomba culture together. It defines goomba culture. I've been quoted as saying, "If I couldn't eat, I'd fuckin' die." If the goomba community couldn't eat good, old-fashioned Italian food, the entire culture would die.

No matter what's going on in the goomba's world, there's food. At the center of everything, there's food. The goomba is always thinking about food. The goomba is the kind of guy that gets up from the table, at lunch, to make dinner reservations. The goomba is the kind of guy that when he hears someone has died, asks, "When's the funeral, and where are we going to eat?" The goomba is the kind of guy that would actually never speak to you again if you insulted his mother's cooking.

The food, the meal, is the center of all goomba life.

The day after a goomba wedding, no one sits around talking about how beautiful the bride looked, or where she got her dress, or where the happy couple are going for their honeymoon. Everyone is talking about the food. All the guests are calling each other to rate the evening, and they base their rating on the quality and the quantity of the food.

"The veal was better than at Sal and Angie's."

"I didn't like the meatballs."

"The food wasn't as good as Uncle Louie's wedding, but it was much better than Cousin Artie's."

At the goomba weddings, you remember, no one brings wedding presents. Instead, the guests all come with an envelope containing the *a boost*—which is a cash gift to get the newlyweds started on their journey through life. During some weddings, you can actually see the guests take money out of the *a boost* envelope, if they feel the dinner wasn't really up to their standards. The goomba that serves his wedding guests a cheap dinner is going to take a big financial hit for it. The money will be flying out of those envelopes.

When someone dies, and the funeral announcement is made, the first thing the goomba does is ask, "Do you want to eat before or after?" The funeral is going to be an important event. The goomba is going to be visiting with the grieving family. It could go on for hours. So the goomba calls his friends and makes dinner arrangements. If it's going to be a very long affair, he may make two dinner arrangements. He'll eat before the funeral with one group of friends, and make a date for another meal after the funeral with another.

A great antipast' with some wine. Where's the bread?

At every goomba function, the centerpiece is the food. It doesn't matter if it's an engagement party, a wedding anniversary, a first communion, a bridal shower, a child's first birthday party, a retirement party. Whatever it is, the food is going to be the main thing. First you set the date. Then you rent the hall. Then you get on the phone to the caterer. Before you know who's coming, even, you know what they're going to be eating.

No business is done in the goomba world without food involved, either. If a man wants to discuss business with another man, the first thing he does is suggest a meal. Not until the macaroni's all gone does the business start. When the espresso and the cannoli come out, only then will the goomba say, "So, here's the setup . . ."

When goomba friends of mine want to talk to me about a business deal, they don't say, "Mr. So and So will see you in his office at three o'clock on Wednesday." They say, "Let's get together, have few glasses of wine and a little macaroni." You know it's about business. But first it's about food.

To the goomba, this isn't just about being hungry. Or about being polite. It's about wanting to do business well. You know you're going to feel closer to someone after you've broken bread with them. It's easier to do business with friends. After you eat, you're more likely to be friends. So the business is more likely to go well.

Even if you're not a goomba, you know this is true, because you've seen the goomba movies. Whether it's *The Godfather, GoodFellas* or *Analyze This,* you've noticed that there is always food around. And the business at hand always comes after the food is eaten.

Even when Michael Corleone makes the date to avenge the shooting of his father in *The Godfather,* he makes the date for an Italian restaurant. And only *after* the meal does he go to the bathroom, retrieve the hidden pistol, and start shooting.

In real goomba life, you hear everyone say, "Let's go have lunch." No one says, "I'll meet you at Starbucks." We don't do that. We don't do business over a $5 coffee in a paper cup. We make a date for lunch, or we make a date for dinner. We sit down at a nice place, on 18th Avenue in Brooklyn, or on Mulberry Street in Little Italy, and we have a nice espresso and a Sambucca and a little pastry. That's how business gets done.

It all starts with the family. In most goomba households, the family dinner is the most important time of the day. The father is working. The mother is running the house. The children are in school, or running wild in the streets. The grandparents, who live in the basement apartment, who knows what they do all day? The grandfather is drinking coffee at the social club. The grandmother is playing gin rummy with the other old ladies, or maybe she's got a numbers racket on the side.

When six o'clock comes, they're all at the table. The family dinner hour is here, and nobody's going to be missing that. This is where everything important happens. This is how the goomba family sticks together. The glue is the macaroni and the gravy.

In a lot of families, the meal is actually eaten in the basement. That's where the grandparents live. And the grandmother is often the best or the most respected cook in the family. So, she's serving at her table.

Whether the family is rich or poor, whether the father is a plumber or a policeman or a company president, the goomba family sits down for dinner together every night. The only variation on this is Friday, Saturday, or Sunday. On Friday, some goombas take their wives or their whole families out for dinner. Same time, same meal, different location. On Saturday, some goombas go out with the guys—or with the guys and their girlfriends. And on Sunday, the goomba is at home again. This time the meal is earlier in the day, and there are more people at the table. Here come the brothers and sisters, and uncles and cousins, and their wives and families.

But whatever it is, there is a meal on the table right in the middle of it.

As a result, food ends up being the most important thing in the fabric of the goomba life. It's tied to everything—especially love and family.

I went to a restaurant in New York recently. It's been there a hundred years. I ordered a *spedini*—a thing that's like fried mozzarella with anchovies. I put my fork in my mouth and bang! The instant I tasted it, I was back with my grandmother. I was sitting at her table, with my fork in her *spedini*. I haven't eaten that dish in over twenty-five years but the instant I tasted it, the years melted away and I was sitting with my grandmother.

There's another place in New York that makes an eggplant parmigiana that tastes exactly like my mother's eggplant parmigiana. I don't know what it is—the cheese, the sauce, the eggplant, the spices—but it tastes *exactly* like hers. How many places have I eaten eggplant parmigiana? About ten thousand. But this one is the one that tastes *exactly* like my mother's. When I sit in that place it's like I'm a little boy sitting down to dinner with my mother. And I feel that love all around me.

I've even got good memories of my father that I associate with food. (I don't have hardly any good memories of my father. But I got this.) He used to make a shrimp dish. He called it "Shrimp Oreganata." He made it with bread crumbs, garlic, and oregano. He made it every Christmas Eve. Now that I'm a goomba father, I make the same dish, for my children. It's part of my childhood tradition, and I'm making it part of their childhood tradition.

Between a man and a woman, sometimes the best times you remember are all tied up with the food you ate. My wife and I still talk about a particular romantic dinner we had one time in New York. It was a freezing night, and we sat in this little joint eating a great meal and having a nice bottle of red wine. Outside it was snowing. Inside it was toasty and warm. We still talk about that night.

Years ago there was a seafood restaurant on the island of Kauai that my wife liked very much—maybe *too* much. One week, she got a little crazy and insisted we had to go there three times. When we got back to the mainland, she discovered she was pregnant with our first daughter. Those meals now seem like three of the most important events of our life together.

Because of all this, the goomba can be very particular about what he eats and where he eats it. The goomba will hardly ever eat at the home of a stranger.

The goomba doesn't usually invite someone to his home unless he already knows that person really well. The goomba home isn't an open house. The goomba doesn't say, "Sure, bring all your friends." The home is for family and close friends only. I have to know someone a long, long time before I have them to the house for a meal. You can know a goomba for years and never see the inside of his place. When a goomba does invite you to the house, this is a big thing. It's a sign of real respect. Most goomba families keep to themselves or their relatives.

This doesn't mean an empty table, though. You've got Aunt Angie and Uncle Carlo everywhere you go. There's cousins everywhere you look. So the goomba gets uncomfortable when he's forced to eat with strangers, or when he has to eat anything he hasn't been served twice a week since he could walk.

I remember one time my wife and I had to go to this baptism or christening or whatever for this friend of my wife's. He was a great guy, Chinese guy, that she worked with. And I guess it's a big tradition for the Chinese to have a party for the name-giving ceremony. So we're there, and everyone's having drinks, and it's all very nice until it's time to eat. We sit down, and these waitresses start to bring out this stuff that I can't even tell what it is. Fish head? Pig's ass? There's not an egg roll in sight. My wife is gagging on this thing that looked like eye of newt. Finally I got up and excused myself. I couldn't do it.

Unfortunately I've had that experience more than once. I remember the first time I ate in a non-goomba household. I went home for dinner with this friend of mine from school. Not an

Italian. His mother had prepared dinner. We sat down and the first course began. It was this plate of limp celery sticks smeared with peanut butter. I thought it was some kind of joke. I thought it was like *Candid Camera.* They couldn't be serious. This is dinner?

Another night, years later, my wife and I went to dinner with these people we didn't know all that well. We thought we were going to pick them up and all go out to a restaurant. But when we got there, they had dinner all prepared. It was some kind of a Mexican-theme thing. Which is fine. But as we were sitting down, the lady realized she was missing a salad plate. She told me, "Steve, would you go in the kitchen and grab one more plate?" So I went in the kitchen. I can't find a plate. All I see is these filthy dirty dishes around the sink. I'm trying to figure out what to do when the lady comes in and says, "Give me one of those." I pick up this filthy dish and give it to her. She wipes it with a paper towel and goes and puts it on the table.

I couldn't eat a bite. And I almost got whiplash trying to gesture to my wife that she shouldn't touch her food, either.

If I had been able to talk to her, I would have used the word *skeeve.* This is a very goomba word. It's a way of saying something makes you sick or disgusted. As in, "I skeeve that place," or "I skeeve the food."

You'll hear goombas say things like, "The floor in that pizzeria is all sticky. I skeeve that." Or, "Why doesn't she ever wash her hair, the skeeve?" Or, "He picks his nose constantly, the skeevey bastard."

The weird thing is there's a double standard here. The goomba doesn't want to eat some other person's food. He is never going to like another goomba's cooking as much as his wife's or his mother's. But if a goomba comes to his house, and doesn't eat the food—what an insult!

GOOMBA PERSONAL ADS

I AM: Call me Angelo. It's not my real name.

YOU ARE: A broad who would actually go out with me, and who shares my enthusiasm for food and sex.

MY MOST INTERESTING FEATURE: I can't tell you in writing, but believe me you're going to be pleasantly surprised.

CELEBRITY I RESEMBLE MOST: That chef on the pizza box.

THINGS I CAN'T LIVE WITHOUT: Olive oil. Gravy. That chef on the pizza box.

IN MY BEDROOM YOU'LL FIND: A fifty-gallon drum of olive oil I got at Cosco. The 64-roll package of toilet paper I got at Cosco. The five-pack of track suits I got at Cosco.

FILL IN THE BLANK: Holding my hand *is sexy*. Jerking me off *is sexier*. Being with you *is exciting*. Being with you when you got cannolis *is more exciting*.

Certain foods you only get at certain times, in the goomba world of food. Some foods are only for holidays. The shrimp thing that my father made was only for Christmas Eve. Pizza Rustica was only for Easter. I don't know why. Pizza Rustica is a kind of stuffed pizza. You bake a meat and cheese filling inside two slabs of pizza dough— kind of like a calzone, but shaped more like a quiche or a pie. It's delicious and something you could eat every day, but in goomba families, the only time you ever see it served in the home is for Easter.

All the holidays are celebrated with food, even if there isn't a specific food attached to the holiday. In most goomba homes, for example, Christmas Eve you get only seafood. It's an all-fish dinner.

The appetizer is going to be fried squid, or mussels, or clams. There's going to be a conch salad, with calamari. There's going to be macaroni with lobster sauce. The main course will be a baked fish that's been marinated in olive oil and vinegar.

Some junior goombas hated this. I know my friend Mike says he loved some of these Christmas Eve foods until he found out what they were or saw them before they had been cooked. He loved fried calamari until he saw all those little squids before they got chopped up. He loved snails, too, in the spaghetti sauce but hated watching them take the slimy things out of the shells and wash them in the sink. The snails would crawl up the side of the sink, trying to escape. Disgusting!

The seafood rule was true even in the lower-middle-class goomba homes. Where they found the money for lobster on Christmas Eve, I don't know. It fell off the back of the lobster truck, maybe. But most goomba homes were like this on Christmas Eve.

Same with New Year's Eve. It was always lobster, when I was a kid, on New Year's Eve. I have no idea how anyone could afford lobster, but this is what you saw on a lot of goomba tables when I was young.

Christmas Day might be more traditional. There's going to be lots of meat—a veal parmigiana, a chicken, meat sauce and fried meatballs with the macaroni. There might even be some traditional *amerigan'* stuff on the table, like a turkey or a ham.

Whatever the main course, there's also going to be lots of red wine. Even the kids will be drinking a little glass of red wine diluted with water. Maybe that's why there aren't so many goomba alcoholics. They get exposed to liquor at an early age. Many's the goomba had his gums coated with *anisetta* when he was teething.

For the older generation of goombas, the birthday was not a big deal except for kids. But for the adults, the saint's day was a special day. If your name was Joey, then you celebrated on St. Joseph's Day. You might have a little party, or a special dinner. But you wouldn't celebrate on your birthday, with presents and all. That was kid stuff. Adults had the saint's day to celebrate. If you were named Joseph, you celebrated March 19. If you were named Michael, you had a little party September 29. There's no Saint Steve, so I didn't have a party on my saint's day.

On Father's Day, the goomba dad is treated like a king. On the table is his favorite meal. Maybe he's veal man. Maybe he's a shrimp man. Maybe he prefers chicken. Maybe it's a beef *bracciole*. Whatever it is, the goomba wife knows it's his favorite, and there's going to be a big spread come Father's Day. He's going to have stuffed artichokes, or rice balls, or fried meatballs, and all the other things he loves.

The opposite, unfortunately, is not always true on Mother's Day. The goomba father may know how to make Shrimp Oreganata. He may know how to barbecue sausages or grill a steak, but he ain't up to making an entire meal. Many a goomba mother has had to spend Mother's Day in the kitchen preparing her own big dinner. But all the children are there, and the husband is on his best behavior. And they all swear the eggplant parmigiana is the best they ever tasted.

And they're right. I think the secret to long life for some Italian women might be the cooking. I know some older Italian women—I mean, women in their 70s and 80s and up—who still spend their entire day cooking. I have a friend whose grandmother makes her own pizza, including the dough, by hand, once a week. I have another friend whose grandmother makes her own pasta. He goes over to her house and helps her roll the dough out and cut it into noodles and lay it out to dry. I have another friend whose grandmother still makes her own *zeppoli*, which is kind of like a fried

Italian doughnut—fried dough, sprinkled with confectioner's sugar.

Unfortunately, the same cooking is probably the secret to a *short* life for a lot of Italian men. You eat like that everyday, boom! It's like a heart attack on a plate. Something's gotta give.

GOING PRO

THERE'S ONE more thing goombas love. It's sex. Since we've covered it in various other ways in various other chapters, I'm not going to say much more about it. But the fact is a lot of goombas love sex. And for a lot of those goombas, loving sex means loving hookers.

There you go. It's out. A lot of goombas love hookers. Or strippers. Which are just hookers with a different business plan. Either way, it's an exchange of sex for money. The hooker is honest about it—you give me this, I give you that. The stripper is more of a tease. You give me this, I'll show you that. You take me out and give me more, maybe, just *maybe*, I'll give you more. The hooker is just an honest working girl. The stripper, she's got larceny in her heart. She'll take your kids' college fund without blinking. I know guys who've wrecked themselves dating strippers.

I'm not saying it's right, either way. It's kind of sleazy, either way. But it happens a lot, with single guys who are new to Las Vegas, for example. And it happens a lot with married guys, who maybe aren't getting what they want in the sack at home. With most of the guys, it's a simple transaction and it's not too disruptive. With the hooker, you're in, you're out, it's a straight business thing. It's quick, it's over, and no one gets hurt.

Not with the strippers. Maybe it's because of the way they work. They dance in these clubs. They're up on the stage. They got 500 guys drooling all over them. They think they're movie stars up there. And, while they're dancing, I guess they are.

They act like *stars*. And they expect to be treated like stars. They'll only go to the most expensive restaurants. They'll only accept the most expensive gifts. You don't drive a $60,000 car? Forget it. You can't play.

There was a story about a guy who fell in love with a stripper. He was very rich, but he was married. And she had a boyfriend. This guy fell for her hard anyway. He was ready to abandon his wife and family. But the girl and her boyfriend saw an opportunity. The boyfriend threatened to kidnap and kill the guy's family if he didn't cough up some huge sum of money. And he was going to do it in some way that would frame the wealthy guy and make it look like he did the murders.

The guy wasn't stupid, and he wasn't a complete weasel. So he came up with the money. That got the boyfriend off his back. But he was still in love with the girl. He eventually dumped his wife and family and moved in with the stripper. Last I heard, he was broke. And alone. When the money ran out, the stripper walked out.

What the hell is that? Maybe the guy never got laid right. He ran into that stripper, and she rocked his world in some wild new way, and he was never right again.

That must happen a lot. I look around Las Vegas society, and I see all these guys with money who are on their second marriages. And the second marriages are always to these strippers, or dancers, or cocktail waitresses, that the guys met when they moved to town. They dump the first wife and marry the tramp, and now the tramp is a Vegas society broad. They're all members of the Junior League and the Ladies Auxiliary. Ten minutes ago they had guys sticking hundred-dollar bills in their G-strings. Now they're running the charity bazaar. Either way, it's the guy that's paying for it.

EPILOGUE

It's Curtains . . .

*S*o, what can I tell you? That's the whole story. Now when you hear the question, "Who wrote the book of love?" you know the answer: The goomba wrote the book of love.

The average goomba knew this already. The average non-goomba probably had his suspicions. The goomba might be a bit of a slob, a bit of a crook, or a bit of a Mafia don, but deep down he's a guy with a lot of love in his heart. Just look at the pictures of the men in this book! See that twinkle in their eyes? That's what I'm talking about. Goomba love!

That twinkle could mean a lot of things. With some of the guys, it's romantic love, or the love of sex. Other guys, it's the love of food or cars or clothes or money or gambling. Other guys, it's the love they feel for their children or their parents or their best friends.

No matter what's behind it, it's goomba love.

It comes in many forms. For example, look what happened to my friend Frank.

Frank's brother-in-law—his sister's husband—was planning a trip to Las Vegas, where Frank lives. He told Frank he was having problems with his marriage—problems in the sex department. He said, "I can't get a blow job."

Frank told him, "No problem!" When his brother-in-law arrived, Frank set him up with a hooker.

The brother-in-law had a great time. When he got back home, he started telling everybody what Frank did for him. He told so many people that his wife found out.

So she called Frank—remember, this is her own brother—and started screaming. "You got my husband a hooker? You got my husband a blow job? Are you insane?"

Frank came right back at her, "Me? I'm trying to save your marriage! You won't give your husband a blow job! Do you want him to leave you?"

Well, the woman must've got the point. A few months later, she was wearing a beautiful new mink coat. It was a gift from her husband: *She started giving him what he wanted.*

Frank said, "From now on, every married guy that comes out here, I'm getting him a blow job. The ones with smart wives will end up buying them mink coats."

There you go. That's goomba love in many different forms. Frank didn't turn his back on his brother-in-law. The brother-in-law didn't leave his wife for the hooker. The wife didn't tell her husband he was a pervert and file for divorce. Everyone did the right thing, and everyone lived happily ever after.

I wish the same for everyone who reads this book—minus the hooker, of course. I hope everyone's life is filled with lots of goomba love, and that everyone lives happily ever after.